SPECIAL  WORLD AND PRESS

Pressetexte auf Abiturniveau

| Photo: *GettyImages*

CARL ED. SCHÜNEMANN KG

CONTENT

Liebe Leserin, lieber Leser,

mit der Reihe **Special World and Press** bieten wir Ihnen eine Sammlung mit Presse-texten zu lehrplanrelevanten Themen des Englischunterrichts an. Die Reihe versteht sich als Sonderpublikation zu unserer Sprachzeitung **World and Press**. Zu einzelnen abitur-relevanten und aktuellen Themen sind original Zeitungsartikel in einer Sammlung zusammengestellt.

Dieses Special ist eine Sammlung original journalistischer Texte und grafischem Material rund um das Thema **Black Lives Matter.** Das Heft richtet sich an Lernende des Sprachniveaus B2 – C2 und ist daher vor allem in der gymnasialen Oberstufe auch in Vorbereitung auf das Englischabitur gewinnbringend einzusetzen.

Original Pressetexte aus *dem Guardian, der Los Angeles Times, der Chicago Tribune* und vielen anderen geben fundierte Einblicke in die Anfänge der Bewegung und wer ihre Gründerinnen sind. Ebenso erfahren die Leserinnen und Leser, auf welche Weise **Black Lives Matter** Einfluss auf Politik und Gesellschaft hat und nicht nur in den USA, sondern auch in Großbritannien und weltweit mit Berechtigung gehört werden will und auch muss. **Informative Grafiken** und **journalistisches Bildmaterial** runden das Angebot ab.

Wie in unserer **Sprachzeitung World and Press** werden jeweils am Ende der Texte die Vokabeln erläutert. Anders als in der Zeitung sind die Texte ein- oder zweispaltig abgedruckt, damit für die Lernenden genügend Platz für Notizen am Rand bleibt. Diese Materialsammlung verzichtet bewusst auf Trainingseinheiten und Aufgabenblät-ter, sondern versteht sich als ein thematisch zusammengestelltes Zusatzangebot für den Englischunterricht in der gymnasialen Oberstufe.

Und noch ein stilistischer Hinweis

Die Schreibweise einiger Wörter sowie die Regeln für Interpunktion sind im britischen und amerikanischen Englisch nicht immer gleich. Außerdem haben viele Zeitungen ihren eigenen Stil, sodass wir versucht haben, diese Stilunterschiede so weit wie möglich beizubehalten.

Einer der Hauptunterschiede ist „**black**" und „**Black**". Im amerikanischen Englisch hat sich der Trend durchgesetzt, „**Black**" großzuschreiben. Im britischen Englisch wird oft die Kleinschreibung verwendet: „**black**". In beiden Sprachen wird „**white**" klein-geschrieben.

Da es sich bei den Texten um Abdrucke aus britischen und amerikanischen Zeitungen handelt, haben wir uns dafür entschieden, die Artikel in den Originalsprachen zu belassen, in denen sie verfasst wurden.

Wir wünschen einen interessanten sowie anregenden Unterricht
und natürlich viel Spaß!

Ihr Sprachzeitungsteam

Black Lives Matter: What It Is, What It Stands for.

ACTIVISM Lost in the controversy around the movement is a sense of what it actually stands for, writes Ryan W. Miller.

A protester *at a demonstration in July 2013 against the acquittal of George Zimmerman in the killing of unarmed Florida teen Trayvon Martin.* | PHOTO: *Getty Images*

1 AFTER A WEEK of conflict in the United States that included the police-involved shooting deaths of Alton Sterling and Philando Castile and the subsequent sniper attack that left five Dallas police officers dead, the Black Lives Matter movement once again has been at the center of controversy. But lost in the discussion is a sense of what Black Lives Matter is and what it stands for.

What is Black Lives Matter?

2 Black Lives Matter was founded by Patrisse Cullors, Alicia Garza, and Opal Tometi as both a hashtag and a political project after the acquittal of George Zimmerman in the 2012 killing of Trayvon Martin. Distraught at the verdict, Oakland, California, community activist Alicia Garza wrote an impassioned Facebook plea ending with the words "black lives matter." Patrisse Cullors, a community organizer from Los Angeles, shared the Facebook post and put a hashtag in front of those three words. The ideals expressed – the economic, political, and social empowerment of African Americans – resonated nationwide.

3 Since 2013, Black Lives Matter has moved from social media platforms to the streets, morphing into an organization and a movement that gained national recognition during demonstrations after the 2014 police-involved killings of Michael Brown and Eric Garner.

How does Black Lives Matter work?

4 What sets Black Lives Matter apart from other social justice groups, however, is its decentralized approach and reliance almost solely on local, rather than national, leadership. Cullors said organizing is often spontaneous and not directed by one person or group of people. "We don't get (people) onto the streets. They get themselves onto the street," she said.

5 Black Lives Matter is made up of a network of local chapters who operate mostly independently. Chelsea Fuller of the Advancement Project, a nonprofit that works with grassroots justice and race movements, said that local organizing is a powerful way to address poverty, access to housing and jobs, community policing, and other issues that intersect with systemic racism. "We can't affect

---

0-1 **CONTROVERSY** Kontroverse — **movement** Bewegung; s.w.u. **grassroots m.** Basisbewegung — **police-involved** mit Polizeibeteiligung — **subsequent** ('sʌbsɪkwənt) folgend — **sniper** ('snaɪpə) Heckenschütze(-in) — **to leave s.o. dead** jdn. das Leben kosten

2-3 **acquittal** (ə'kwɪtəl) Freispruch — **distraught at** (dɪ'strɔːt) bestürzt über — **verdict** ('--) Urteil — **impassioned** (ɪm'pæʃənd) leidenschaftlich — **plea** (pliː) Plädoyer — **social empowerment** gesellschaftliche Stärkung — **to resonate** ('rezəneɪt) Widerhall finden — **to morph into s.th.** (mɔːf) s. in etw. verwandeln — **recognition** (,rekəg'nɪʃən) Anerkennung; Bekanntheit

4 **to set o.s. apart from s.th.** s. von etw. unterscheiden — **social justice** soziale Gerechtigkeit — **reliance** (rɪ'laɪəns) Verlass; Abhängigkeit — **solely** ('səʊlli) ausschließlich — **spontaneous** (spɒn'teɪnɪəs) — **to direct** lenken; führen

5 **to be made up of** bestehen aus — **chapter** Ortsgruppe — **nonprofit** (-'--) gemeinnützige Organisation — **to address s.th.** etw. thematisieren — **housing** Wohnraum — **policing** Polizeiarbeit — **to intersect** s. überschneiden — **systemic racism** institutioneller Rassismus — **narrative** ('nærətɪv) Erzählung; Narrativ — **legislation** (,ledʒɪ'sleɪʃən) Gesetze — **to come down** h.: erlassen werden — **to push back** s. wehren — **to take a stand** Stellung beziehen

6-8 **directive** Richtlinie; h.: Zielsetzung — **dignity** ('dɪgnəti) Würde — **affiliated** (ə'fɪlieɪtɪd) angegliedert — **conception** Annahme; s.w.u. **misconception** Fehlannahme; Missverständnis — **to condemn s.th.** (kən'dem) etw. verurteilen — **counter to s.th.** im Widerspruch zu etw. — **to accomplish** erreichen — **claim** Behauptung — **direction** Richtung; Orientierung — **leaderless** führungslos; **leaderful** führungsstark

national narrative, and we can't affect national legislation that comes down and affects local people if local people don't push back and take a stand about what's happening in local communities," Fuller said.

What does Black Lives Matter stand for?

6   The most important directive of Black Lives Matter, Cullors said, is to deal with anti-black racism, to "push for black people's right to live with dignity and respect" and be included in the American democracy that they helped create.

7   "This is about the quality of life for black people, for poor people in this country," said Umi Selah, co-director of Dream Defenders in Miami. Though not officially affiliated, Dream Defenders and similar social justice groups often align themselves with Black Lives Matter. "The conception that all we're mad about is police and policing is a strong misconception," Selah said. In fact, Black Lives Matter released a statement last week condemning the shooting in Dallas as counter to what the movement is trying to accomplish.

8   Cullors also hears claims that Black Lives Matter lacks direction or strategy. But Cullors said the strategy is clear – working to ensure that black people live with the full dignity of their human rights. "We are not leaderless. We're leaderful," she said. "We're trying to change the world … developing a new vision for what this generation of black leaders can look like."

From left to right: *Patrisse Cullors, Opal Tometi, and Alicia Garza pose with an award during the 2016 Glamour Women of the Year Awards.* | PHOTO: *Getty Images*

Why Activists Brought the Black Lives Matter Movement to the UK

UNITED KINGDOM
Tracy McVeigh explains how a protest movement first launched in America made its mark in Britain.

1   ON THE SAME day last week as protesters lay down in front of traffic on roads around England, a video of the shooting of an unarmed teenager by police in Chicago was released in the United States. Shock and anger greeted the death of 18-year-old Paul O'Neal, and sympathy poured in for his family.

2   Some 4,000 miles away, the peaceful protest being played out on the asphalt, the first ever day of action by Black Lives Matter UK, met with disbelief and irritation and a handful of arrests. Why were motorists being inconvenienced over a racism that was America's problem?

3   There lay the British complacency, said Natalie Jeffers, co-founder of Black Lives Matter UK. There might be fewer guns used in the UK, she said, "but there is a war going on against black people".

4   Her words are supported by statistics showing an alarming gulf between the experiences of black and white people in Britain – in education, in the justice and prison systems, and in employment. Stop and search is heavily targeted at young black men – who are four times more likely to be stopped by police than young white men – while people from black and ethnic minorities are far more likely to go to prison than a white person committing a similar offence.

5   In 2014, black people made up 10% of the total prison population, while making up 3.5% of the UK's total population, according to the Equality and Human Rights Commission. There is a greater disparity between the proportion of black people in prison and in the general population than there is in the US.   ➔

0–1   **MOVEMENT** Bewegung; s.w.u. **liberation m.** Befreiungsbewegung — **to make one's mark** h.: Fuß fassen — **protester** Demonstrant(in) — **unarmed** unbewaffnet — **to greet** h.: auslösen — **sympathy poured in** ('sɪmpəθi) die Anteilnahme war groß

2–3   **to play out** s. abspielen — **on the asphalt** ('æsfɔːlt) auf der Straße — **to meet with s.th.** auf etw. stoßen — **disbelief** (ˌdɪsbɪ'liːf) Unglaube — **irritation** Irritation; Verärgerung — **to inconvenience s.o.** (ˌɪnkən'viːniəns) jdm. Unannehmlichkeiten bereiten — **complacency** (kəm'pleɪsənsi) Selbstgefälligkeit — **co-founder** Mitbegründer(in)

4–5   **gulf** Kluft — **stop and search** Polizeipraxis, bei der eine Person angehalten und durchsucht wird — **to target s.o.** auf jdn. abzielen — **ethnic minority** (maɪ'nɒrəti) e. Minderheit — **to make up** h.: stellen; bilden — **equality** (iˈkwɒləti) Gleichberechtigung — **disparity** Missverhältnis — **proportion** Anteil; s.w.u. **disproportionate** (ˌdɪsprə'pɔːʃənət) überproportional

Protesters in support *of the Black Lives Matter movement during the Million People March from Notting Hill to Hyde Park in London in August 2020.* | PHOTO: *Getty Images*

6 Research by the campaign group Inquest shows a disproportionate number of those who have died as a result of the use of force in police custody were black or from minority ethnic groups. Despite numerous scandals over abuse at immigration detention centres and allegations of brutality used during deportations, no criminal charges have ever been brought against anyone.

7 It suggested a radically different picture, said Jeffers, of the kind of equality in British society than many like to paint. "We have dozens of British families left fighting for justice over their loved ones suffering state violence, so we know there's a problem in the UK, and that's before the Brexit debate that we're now seeing reflected in the rise in racism at street level," said Jeffers. …

8 "We really are focused on sharing the British narrative," said Jeffers. "It might have taken the shocking images from deaths in the US to awaken young people, but they're aware of oppression at an individual household level. They see what happens within our communities. After Brexit, people are seeing the direct change in language online, aware of being seen as another in your own country. People of colour are even being told to 'go home'. There were vans bearing racist slogans being driven round British streets. We know there's a direct link between street racism and state racism.

9 "When you are walking around the streets of the UK as a black or brown person, you're seeing this; you're feeling this. It's an everyday occurrence. It's been too often silenced by the national narrative of where the UK is at. But we know the black and ethnic minority community was hit twice as hard by austerity as everyone else. We know a black woman is more likely to be unemployed than a white woman.

10 "In Britain, somebody dies every six days in police custody, not just black people. But black people are over-represented in these cases. As is mental health – if a black man has a mental health episode, police are more likely to see that as a show of aggression than if a white person has the same episode."

11 Jeffers, from Birmingham, lost her brother, Luke, a 42-year-old schizophrenic, under tragic circumstances when his condition worsened after he lost his benefits. It is not clear how he died. "For him, it was bureaucratic violence," she said. "It's not all about deaths. Look at Julian Cole, [a young black man] left in an unresponsive state in Bedfordshire, left with a broken neck. They said he was drunk, then back came the toxicology, and he wasn't. … Of 1,563 deaths in police custody since 1990, we have zero convictions." …

12 Jeffers said the gun-driven brutality in the US was obviously not being replicated on the streets of Britain, but inequality and discrimination existed at alarming levels. Black Lives Matter in the US began initially as a hashtag on social media in 2013 after the acquittal of George Zimmerman, who killed unarmed teenager Trayvon Martin. Co-founders Alicia Garza, Patrisse Cullors, and Opal Tometi said they wanted to rebuild a black liberation movement but one led by the most marginalised, giving a voice to women, to gay, and transgender people.

13 That, said Jeffers, was the same principle for the UK movement. "BLM UK gives us a new framework. Nobody is excluded from the room. But we have learned it's important not to see the movement go the way a lot of anti-racist movements do, led by white people, middle-class white people. We welcome white allies, and we want participation, but please do not take over from people who are directly affected by the oppression and acknowledge your privilege. Listen, but don't dilute or devolve what is being said. Silence, white silence, is complicity, and there is room for everyone to engage in change. We can be a powerful force. … A lot of people have lost their voice; they feel powerless. We want to give them their voice back."

© 2016 Guardian News and Media Ltd

---

⁶⁻⁷ **research** Recherchen — **campaign group** Initiative — **police custody** (ˈkʌstədi) Polizeigewahrsam — **numerous** (ˈnjuːmərəs) zahlreich — **immigration detention centre** Abschiebehaftanstalt — **allegation** (æləˈgeɪʃən) Vorwurf — **deportation** Abschiebung — **to bring criminal charges** Strafanzeige erstatten — **loved ones** Nahestehende
⁸⁻⁹ **to share** vermitteln — **narrative** (ˈnærətɪv) Erzählung; Narrativ — **to awake** (əˈweɪk) h.: aufrütteln — **oppression** Unterdrückung — **people of colour** Menschen, die nicht weiß sind — **to bear** tragen — **everyday occurrence** (əˈkʌrəns) alltägliches Ereignis — **s.th. is being silenced** etw. wird verschwiegen — **austerity** (ɔːˈsterəti) h.: Sparpolitik
¹⁰⁻¹¹ **episode** h.: (Krankheits)Episode — **show of aggression** Ausdruck von Aggression — **schizophrenic** (ˌskɪtsəˈfrenɪk) Schizophrene(r) — **to worsen** (ˈwɜːsən) s. verschlechtern — **benefits** Sozialleistungen — **bureaucratic** (ˌbjʊərəˈkrætɪk) bürokratisch — **unresponsive** (ˌʌnrɪˈspɒnsɪv) nicht ansprechbar — **toxicology** (ˌtɒksɪˈkɒlədʒi) h.: toxikologische Untersuchung — **conviction** Verurteilung
¹² **gun-driven** durch Waffengewalt verursacht — **to replicate** nachahmen — **inequality** Ungleichheit — **acquittal** (əˈkwɪtəl) Freispruch — **the marginalised** (ˈmaːdʒɪnəlaɪzd) die Ausgegrenzten — **to give a voice to s.o.** jdm. e-e Stimme geben
¹³ **principle** Grundprinzip — **framework** (fig) Rahmen — **to exclude** (ɪkˈskluːd) ausschließen — **to go the way of** s. in eine Richtung entwickeln — **ally** (ˈælaɪ) Verbündete(r) — **participation** Beteiligung — **to acknowledge** (əkˈnɒlɪdʒ) anerkennen — **to dilute** (daɪˈluːt) verwässern; h.: verzerren — **to devolve** h.: (fig) verdrehen — **complicity** (kəmˈplɪsəti) Mittäterschaft — **to engage in s.th.** s. für etw. einsetzen — **force** Kraft — **powerless** machtlos

Housing the Homeless, Feeding School Children

SOCIETY Nicquel Terry Ellis writes about how Black families devastated by police violence are fighting to end racism.

Bridgett Floyd, *George Floyd's sister, speaks during the March on Washington at the Lincoln Memorial on August 28, 2020, in Washington, DC.*

Civil rights attorney *Benjamin Crump.* | PHOTOS: *Getty Images*

1 WHEN Black Lives Matter protests erupted across the country following George Floyd's death, Bridgett Floyd thought the show of support would mark an end to police violence against Black people. But two weeks later, Rayshard Brooks was fatally shot by an Atlanta police officer. Two months after that, Jacob Blake was shot in the back seven times by a Kenosha police officer.

2 "To continually turn on the TV and see police brutality is still being done, there has to be a change," said Bridgett Floyd, who is George Floyd's younger sister. Bridgett Floyd sprung into action. She and her siblings launched the George Floyd Memorial Foundation in September, joining a growing movement of Black families devastated by police brutality and racist violence who are fighting to end the unjust treatment of people of color.

3 The families have created foundations to lobby for police reform, racial equality, and investment in Black and brown neighborhoods and provide a support system for each other. They've stood on the frontlines of the fight for racial justice, often holding back tears as they speak out at protests, press conferences, and meetings with officials.

4 Black Americans are three times more likely than white Americans to be killed by police, according to a study published this year by the Harvard T.H. Chan School of Public Health.

5 Advocacy, the families say, is often part of the grieving process. After facing the hurt, they have a desire to keep their loved one's legacy alive and prevent more Black families from experiencing the same grief. "We pretty much want to be on the frontlines to help fight systemic racism," Bridgett Floyd said. "And being that my brother isn't here to be the voice that people need to hear, we are going to make sure that we (are) that voice by promoting global awareness and peaceful protests for justice and police brutality."   ➔

0–1   **TO HOUSE** unterbringen — **the homeless** die Obdachlosen — **to devastate s.th.** ('devəsteıt) etw. zerstören — **to erupt** (ı'rʌpt) ausbrechen — **show** h.: Bekundung — **to mark** bedeuten

2   **continually** (kən'tınjuəli) andauernd — **police brutality** polizeiliche Übergriffe — **to spring into action** aktiv werden — **siblings** Geschwister — **memorial foundation** Gedenkstiftung — **movement** Bewegung — **unjust** (-'-) ungerecht; s.w.u. **injustice** (ın'dʒʌstıs) Ungerechtigkeit — **people of color** Menschen, die nicht weiß sind

3–4   **to lobby for s.th.** s. für etw. einsetzen — **to stand on the frontlines** (fig) an vorderster Front stehen — **to hold back** zurückhalten — **to speak out** das Wort ergreifen — **official** Regierungsmitarbeiter(in)

5   **advocacy** ('ædvəkəsi) Lobbyarbeit — **grieving process** ('gri:vıŋ) Trauerprozess; s.w.u. **to grieve** trauern — **hurt** Schmerz — **to keep s.o.'s legacy alive** ('legəsi) jds. Vermächtnis bewahren — **loved one** Angehörige(r) — **systemic racism** institutioneller Rassismus — **being that ...** angesichts der Tatsache, dass ... — **voice** (fig) Sprachrohr; s.w.u. **to find one's voice** die Sprache wiederfinden — **to promote s.th.** etw. fördern — **awareness** (ə'weənəs) Bewusstsein

6 Bridgett Floyd said she created the George Floyd Memorial Foundation to bridge the gap between the community and law enforcement. It strives to propose police reform, engage in protests, encourage voting, host community events, educate the public on racial injustice, and open centers that will be safe havens for young Black men. Bridgett Floyd said she also wants to create a second-chance program that provides services for men and women released from prison.

7 The Floyd family officially launched the foundation during a National Homeless Day event in Minneapolis on Sept. 13. At the event, the family presented a $5,000 donation to the Salvation Army Harbor Light Center where George Floyd worked.

8 Benjamin Crump, a prominent civil rights attorney who represents several Black families changed forever by police violence, including the Floyds, said the launch event was fitting because George Floyd was known as a selfless man who would take homeless people to medical appointments and basketball games.

9 Crump said he, too, thought the global response to George Floyd's death would lead to better police relations in the Black community. "I still thought George's case was one of such proportion that police were going to stop, at least for a while, killing us," Crump told USA TODAY. "But that's not the case, and we've got work to do, and that's why the (George Floyd) foundation is needed more than ever."

10 Some Black families crushed by racist violence and police brutality this year are gradually finding their voice. Wanda Cooper-Jones, whose son, Ahmaud Arbery, was chased and killed by three white men on Feb. 23 as he jogged through a southern Georgia neighborhood, spoke at the Commitment March on Washington and joined Breonna Taylor protests in Louisville this summer. "I thought about the days after Ahmaud was killed, and I was surrounded by family," Cooper-Jones said in an interview with USA TODAY. "But no one I was surrounded by could feel what I was going through. And it was important to be around someone who could feel the same pain."

11 Cooper-Jones said she eventually wants to create a foundation that caters to young, Black males. Her goal would be to keep them out of the criminal justice system and on a path to success. "I want to help the youth. I love children," Cooper-Jones said. "But I'm still grieving and trying to get back to normal."

12 Fighting for justice has bonded many Black families together. Cephus Johnson, Oscar Grant's uncle, recalled being angry after Grant's death. Witnesses recorded video of the officer shooting Grant in the back as he lay face down on the train platform. "When I saw the video, I could remember collapsing," Johnson said, adding that he was shocked to see such unjust treatment of a Black person in a nation where everyone should be created equal. In 2014, he founded Families United 4 Justice – a network of Black people who have lost family members to police brutality or racist violence. The non-profit's main goals are police accountability and holistic support services for its families.

13 Families United 4 Justice hosts a conference every year where families gather for workshops on dealing with the media, telling their story, and the history of policing among other topics. "Everybody knows now that something has to be done," Johnson said. "Because there is a real internal struggle within this country when it comes to the state and the people. And the people are suffering at the hands of the police."

14 Valerie Castile, whose son, Philando Castile, was fatally shot by a Minneapolis police officer in 2016, also wanted to help other families hurt by police brutality. Castile said after accepting that she would never get her son back, she founded the Philando Castile Relief Foundation in 2018. The organization offers meals, grief counseling services, funeral attire, and grocery store gift cards for families.

15 The foundation also strives to end child hunger. Since it launched, the organization has paid off more than $150,000 in school lunch debt for students in Minneapolis-St. Paul area schools, Valerie Castile said. "Our communities are struggling on so many different levels, and what happened to Philando was wrong on so many levels," Valerie Castile said. "I had to take time to look at the overall big picture. It's very important that we stand with our community because we have been oppressed for so long."

6–7 **to bridge the gap** die Kluft überbrücken — **law enforcement** (ɪnˈfɔːsmənt) Polizei — **to strive to do s.th.** (straɪv) bestrebt sein, etw. zu tun — **to engage in s.th.** s. an etw. beteiligen — **to host** veranstalten — **safe haven** (fig) sicherer Hafen — **Salvation Army** Heilsarmee
8–10 **prominent** ('---) bekannt — **civil rights attorney** (əˈtɜːni) Bürgerrechtsanwalt(-anwältin) — **to represent** (ˌreprɪˈzent) vertreten — **launch event** (lɔːntʃ) Auftaktveranstaltung — **fitting** passend — **selfless** selbstlos — **proportion** (fig) Ausmaß — **to crush** (fig) erdrücken — **march** Protestmarsch
11–13 **to cater to s.o.** auf jdn. ausgerichtet sein — **criminal justice system** Strafjustizsystem — **to bond together** (fig) zus.schweißen — **non-profit** gemeinnützige Organisation — **accountability** (əˌkaʊntəˈbɪləti) Rechenschaftspflicht — **policing** Polizeiarbeit — **when it comes to …** was … anbelangt — **to suffer at the hands of s.o.** unter jdm. leiden
14–15 **relief foundation** Hilfsstiftung — **grief counseling** (ˈkaʊnsəlɪŋ) Trauerbegleitung — **funeral attire** (ˈfjuːnərəl; əˈtaɪə) Trauerkleidung — **gift card** Gutschein — **on so many (different) levels** in vielerlei Hinsicht — **to take time** s. Zeit nehmen — **the big picture** das große Ganze — **to stand with s.o.** an jds. Seite stehen — **oppressed** (əˈprest) unterdrückt

Graffiti in Berlin, *depicting George Floyd who died in Minneapolis after a white policeman knelt on his neck for several minutes.* | PHOTO: *Getty Images*

George Floyd Killing: What Sparked the Protests – and What Has Been the Response?

DEATH OF GEORGE FLOYD

Protests have flared up across the US as people demand justice and systemic change to end police brutality, writes Lauren Aratani.

1 THE US IS undergoing a reckoning on race and police brutality after footage went viral of a white police officer killing a black man by kneeling on his neck for more than eight minutes. Protests have flared up across the country as people demand the arrest of the officers involved in the killing and for systemic change that will put an end to police brutality.

What prompted the protests?

2 Protests erupted on Tuesday in Minneapolis, Minnesota, after word got out that George Floyd, 46, a black man, was killed in police custody on Monday night after Derek Chauvin, a white police officer, knelt on his neck. The officers were responding to a call from a grocery store that claimed Floyd used a fake $20 bill. Police said he "physically resisted officers" once police located him inside his car.

3 In graphic footage of the incident shared on social media, Floyd can be heard shouting "I can't breathe" and "Don't kill me!" as the officer contin-

ues to kneel on his neck until medical personnel arrive. On Tuesday, the Minneapolis police department confirmed that he died "a short time" after a "medical incident" once he was transported to hospital.

4 Floyd's family and friends called him a "gentle giant" because he was tall with a "quiet personality but a beautiful spirit". The father of a six-year-old daughter had recently been laid off from his job as a bouncer at a local restaurant.

Have any arrests been made?

5 Chauvin was arrested on Friday afternoon on charges of third-degree murder and second-degree manslaughter. According to the complaint filed by the county prosecutor against Chauvin, Chauvin had his knee on Floyd's neck for eight minutes and 46 seconds total, two minutes and 43 seconds of which Floyd was unresponsive. "Police are trained that this type of restraint with a subject in a prone position is inherently dangerous," the complaint said. ⟳

0–1   **TO SPARK** (fig) entfachen — **to flare up** (fig) aufflammen — **systemic change** Systemwandel — **police brutality** polizeiliche Übergriffe — **to undergo** durchleben — **reckoning** Aufarbeitung; Auseinandersetzung — **(video) footage** ('fʊtɪdʒ) Videoaufnahmen — **to go viral** s. rasend schnell verbreiten

2–4   **to prompt s.th.** etw. auslösen — **to erupt** (ɪ'rʌpt) ausbrechen — **to get the word out** die Nachricht verbreiten — **police custody** ('kʌstədi) Polizeigewahrsam — **to resist** s. widersetzen — **graphic** h.: drastisch — **gentle giant** sanfter Riese — **spirit** Wesen; Seele — **to lay off** entlassen — **bouncer** Türsteher(in)

5   **charge** Vorwurf; s.w.u. **to charge s.o.** jdn. anklagen — **third-degree murder** billigende Inkaufnahme e-r Tötung — **second-degree manslaughter** ('mæn,slɔːtə) fahrlässige Tötung — **complaint** Klage — **to file** einreichen — **prosecutor** ('prɒsɪkjuːtə) Staatsanwaltschaft — **unresponsive** (ˌʌnrɪ'spɒnsɪv) nicht ansprechbar — **restraint** Fixierung; s.w.u. **to restrain s.o.** jdn. fixieren — **subject** Zielperson — **prone position** Bauchlage — **inherently** (ɪn'herəntli) grundsätzlich

Police officers *kneel during a rally in Coral Gables, Florida, in May 2020, in response to the recent death of George Floyd.* | PHOTO: *Getty Images*

6 The complaint also said that the autopsy of Floyd revealed "no physical findings that support a diagnosis of traumatic asphyxia or strangulation". Rather, the "combined effect of Floyd being restrained by the police, his underlying health conditions, and any potential intoxicants in his system likely contributed to his death". The family plans a second, independent autopsy. The arrest came four days after the incident. The officers were fired on Tuesday.

What other incidents sparked the protests?

7 The police killing of George Floyd comes on the back of two other high-profile killings of black Americans in recent weeks. Video footage of the murder of Ahmaud Arbery, 25, from 23 February began circulating in early May. Arbery was jogging through a neighbourhood outside Brunswick, Georgia, when he was shot dead by two white men, a 64-year-old father and his 34-year-old son, in a pickup truck who were pursuing him. The men were charged with murder and aggravated assault and arrested on 7 May after footage of the incident went viral.

8 Just a few weeks after Arbery died, Breonna Taylor, a 26-year-old certified EMT, was killed in her bed at home by police officers who were serving a "no-knock" warrant for a narcotics investigation on 13 March. Taylor's boyfriend, Kenneth Walker, said he believed he was witnessing a home invasion when police broke down their apartment door. Walker picked up his gun and fired a shot that hit an officer in the leg. In response, officers fired more than 20 times. Taylor was hit eight times and killed.

Where are the protests?

9 Protests have taken place all around the US, as they have since news of Arbery's murder began to spread earlier in May. The killing of Floyd was a tipping point. The largest demonstrations have been in the Twin Cities, Minneapolis and St Paul, where peaceful protests have turned into riots in places following clashes with police. Other protests have taken place in Denver, Chicago, Oakland, Los Angeles, Columbus, and New York.

What's been happening during the protests?

10 "I can't breathe" has become the rallying cry for demonstrators, bringing back a phrase that was used in protests around the police killing of Eric Garner in New York City in 2014.

11 In Minneapolis, hundreds marched on Wednesday from the site of the confrontation between the police officer and Floyd to the police precinct where the officer was based. When the protest reached the police precinct, officers dressed in riot gear clashed with demonstrators. Videos showed protesters throwing rocks and bottles at police vehicles and police officers using teargas, smoke and flash bombs, and rubber bullets. ...

What has the response to the protests been?

12 Just past midnight on Friday morning, Donald Trump tweeted that he sent the National Guard to combat the protests in Minneapolis, criticizing the city's "radical leftist" leaders and threatening a crackdown against demonstrators. "When the looting starts, the shooting starts," the president wrote in a tweet that has since been hidden by Twitter for "glorifying violence".

13 Local leaders have denounced calls for violence against protesters. But in a press conference on Friday, Minnesota's governor, Tim Walz, said that

---

6 findings Befunde — **asphyxia** (əsˈfɪksiə) Erstickung — **strangulation** (ˌstræŋɡjəˈleɪʃən) Strangulation — **underlying** zugrunde liegend — **intoxicant** (ɪnˈtɒksɪkənt) Rauschmittel — **system** h.: Körper
7–8 **to come on the back of s.th.** vor dem Hintergrund von etw. geschehen — **high-profile** im Fokus der Öffentlichkeit stehend — **to circulate** (ˈsɜːkjəleɪt) kursieren — **to pursue s.o.** (pəˈsjuː) jdn. verfolgen — **aggravated assault** (ˌæɡrəveɪtɪd əˈsɒlt) schwere Körperverletzung — **certified** (ˈsɜːtɪfaɪd) staatlich geprüft — **EMT = emergency medical technician** Rettungssanitäter(in) — **to serve** h.: vollziehen — **"no-knock" warrant** (ˈwɒrənt) Durchsuchungsbeschluss, bei dem sich die Polizei nicht durch Anklopfen ankündigen muss — **narcotics** (ˈnɑːkɒtɪks) Rauschgift — **home invasion** Hausfriedensbruch
9–10 **tipping point** Wendepunkt — **riots** (ˈraɪəts) Unruhen; s.w.u. **riot gear** Schutzausrüstung — **in places** stellenweise — **clash** Zus.stoß; s.w.u. **to clash** zus.stoßen — **rallying cry** (ˈrælɪɪŋ) Parole
11–12 **police precinct** (ˈpriːsɪŋkt) Polizeirevier — **teargas** Tränengas — **smoke and flash bombs** Rauch- und Leuchtbomben — **rubber bullet** (ˈbʊlɪt) Gummigeschoss — **to combat** bekämpfen — **radical leftist** linksradikal — **crackdown** hartes Durchgreifen — **looting** Plünderung — **to glorify** (ˈɡlɔːrɪfaɪ) verherrlichen
13–14 **to denounce** (dɪˈnaʊns) verurteilen — **to restore order** die Ordnung wiederherstellen — **societal** (səˈsaɪətəl) gesellschaftlich — **injustice** (ɪnˈdʒʌstɪs) Ungerechtigkeit — **ashes** Asche; Trümmer — **anguish** (ˈæŋɡwɪʃ) Leid — **oppressor** Unterdrücker(in) — **to endanger** gefährden — **urge** (ɜːdʒ) Drang — **to raise one's voice** die Stimme erheben — **unison** (ˈjuːnɪsən) Einklang; Einigkeit — **outrage** (ˈ--) Empörung

restoring order was crucial to begin repairing societal injustices. "The ashes are symbolic of decades and generations of pain and anguish unheard," Walz said. "George Floyd's death should lead to justice and systemic change, not more death and destruction."

14 Floyd's family "told me they want peace in Minneapolis, but they know that black people want peace in their souls and that until we get #JusticeForFloyd there will be no peace," the family's lawyer, Ben Crump, said in a statement. "We also cannot sink to the level of our oppressors and endanger each other as we respond to the necessary urge to raise our voices in unison and outrage."

© 2020 Guardian News and Media Ltd

Protesters *in Los Angeles in June 2020.* | PHOTO: *Picture Alliance*

Black Police Officers See Fight for Racial Justice through Personal Lens

POLICE OFFICERS Black law enforcement leaders tell Alene Tchekmedyian and Nicole Santa Cruz they are uniquely equipped to understand the racism embedded in the criminal justice system.

1 AFTER DAYS of protests over police brutality in Los Angeles County, a young sheriff's deputy on the front lines reached out to her commander, reeling. As a Black woman, she wanted to show solidarity with her community in grieving the brutal police killing of George Floyd. But as a law enforcement officer, she feared backlash from her peers if she were to take a knee. "My comment to her was, if it's genuine, if that's how you feel, we're not going to criticize you," said Cmdr. April Tardy, who also is Black.

2 That personal conflict highlights the delicate duality of being a Black police officer in America during this moment of unrest. In interviews, Black law enforcement leaders said they are uniquely equipped to understand the racism embedded in the criminal justice system, the history of oppression of their community, and how that has sowed decades of distrust of the police. They see themselves in a position to bridge the differences. ⮑

Protestors *have a discussion with a commanding officer in Cleveland, Ohio.* | PHOTO: *Picture Alliance*

---

0   **TO SEE S.TH. through a personal lens** e-e persönliche Sichtweise auf etw. haben (**lens** Linse) — **law enforcement leader** (ınˈfɔːsmənt) Polizeichef(in) — **embedded** (fig) tief verwurzelt — **criminal justice system** Strafjustizsystem

1   **police brutality** polizeiliche Übergriffe — **sheriff's deputy** (ˈdepjəti) Polizeibeamter(-in) — **to reach out to s.o.** s. an jdn. wenden — **commander** h.: Vorgesetzte(r) — **reeling** erschüttert — **to grieve s.th.** (griːv) um etw. trauern — **backlash** Gegenreaktion — **peer** h.: Kollege(-in) — **to take a knee** niederknien (als Geste des friedlichen Protests) — **genuine** (ˈdʒenjuɪn) echt; aufrichtig

2–3   **delicate** (ˈdelɪkət) heikel — **duality** (dʒuːˈæləti) h.: Doppelrolle — **unrest** (-ˈ-) Unruhen — **oppression** Unterdrückung — **to sow** (səʊ) säen; h.: schaffen — **distrust** Misstrauen — **to bridge s.th.** (fig) etw. überbrücken — **to acknowledge** (əkˈnɒlɪdʒ) eingestehen — **to yield s.th.** (jiːld) etw. hervorbringen; h.: zu etw. führen — **to be on the receiving end of s.th.** Opfer von etw. werden — **slur** (slɜː) Beleidigung — **derogatory** (dɪˈrɒgətəri) abwertend

↪ 3   But working within the system, some acknowledge, has not always yielded changes in policies or behavior. And recently, Black officers also have been on the receiving end of racist slurs and derogatory remarks while on the front lines.

4   San Francisco Police Chief Bill Scott said he is deeply aware of and sensitive to both sides of the debate engulfing the nation over racial justice. In an interview, he recounted personal incidents that remain indelible: "For sale" signs going up when his family moved to a mostly white Alabama neighborhood in the 1970s, being in stores where an employee eyed his every move, hearing car doors locking on the street as he walked by. "Growing up in that environment you can't escape the fact that you're Black," he said.

5   Experts said that moving forward requires a culture shift in policing that goes beyond diversifying the ranks and prioritizes honest conversations about long-standing harmful practices. Hiring more officers of color means little if they're not placed in leadership positions or empowered to speak out against wrongdoing, said Rod Brunson, a professor at Northeastern University's School of Criminology and Criminal Justice. "Inclusion is bringing people into an organization and hoping they don't adhere to particularly bad practices but they help to change the culture of policing from within," he said.

6   According to the Pew Research Center, surveys in 2016 of law enforcement officers found that 72% of white officers said the deaths of Black people in America during police encounters were isolated incidents, while 57% of Black officers said they are signs of a systemic problem.

7   But as important as who polices communities is how they're policed, Brunson said. At least two of the officers involved in a widely publicized incident in May in Atlanta where two college students were Tasered were people of color, he noted. One of the four officers charged in Floyd's death is Black. An officer's race "doesn't magically insulate people from poor treatment," Brunson said.

San Francisco *Police Chief Bill Scott.*
| Photo: *Getty Images*

"There's also an organizational demand. So what type of behavior is expected and culture is tolerated and, more importantly, incentivized in police departments?"

8   Charles Ramsey, the former Philadelphia police commissioner who co-chaired President Obama's Task Force on 21st Century Policing, said officers need to see themselves through the eyes of those being policed. At times, Ramsey was criticized by the rank and file for being too harsh in disciplining officers. He believes it's important for officers to understand how police have been used to implement racist policies, such as Jim Crow laws.

9   Negative encounters with police, many current Black officers say, pushed them toward a law enforcement career. As a teenager, Horace Boatwright was walking home from a baseball game in South Carolina when an officer stopped him. "He said if he caught me out at night again, I would not make it home," said Boatwright, now deputy chief of the San Bernardino County Sheriff's Department. "I instantly became fearful of law enforcement." He joined the career to "do my part in modeling what a police officer should be – that's ethical, accountable, and compassionate to the needs of the community."

---

4   **to engulf s.th.** etw. verschlingen; h.: etw. erfassen — **to recount** (rɪ'kaʊnt) erzählen — **indelible** (ɪn'deləbəl) unauslöschlich — **to go up** h.: aufgestellt werden — **to eye s.o./s.th.** jdn./etw. beäugen — **you can't escape the fact that …** man kommt um die Tatsache nicht herum, dass …

5   **to move forward** Fortschritte machen — **shift** Wandel — **policing** Polizeiarbeit; s.w.u. **to police** (polizeilich) kontrollieren — **to diversify** (daɪ'vɜːsɪfaɪ) diversifizieren — **the ranks;** s.w.u. **the rank and file** die Belegschaft — **to prioritize s.th.** (praɪ'ɒrɪtaɪz) etw. Priorität geben — **long-standing** seit Langem bestehend — **officers of color** Polizisten, die nicht weiß sind — **to empower** befähigen — **to speak out against s.th.** s. gegen etw. aussprechen — **wrongdoing** ('-,--) Fehlverhalten — **inclusion** Inklusion — **to adhere to s.th.** (əd'hɪə) s. an etw. halten

6–7   **survey** ('sɜːveɪ) Umfrage — **encounter** Begegnung — **isolated incident** Einzelfall — **widely publicized** ('pʌblɪsaɪzd) vielbeachtet — **to taser s.o.** jdn. tasern — **to insulate s.o. from s.th.** ('ɪnsjəleɪt) jdn. vor etw. schützen — **to incentivize** (ɪn'sentɪvaɪz) (durch Anreize) fördern

8   **police commissioner** (kə'mɪʃənə) Polizeipräsident(in) — **to co-chair** den Co-Vorsitz innehaben — **task force** Arbeitsgruppe — **through the eyes of s.o.** aus der Sicht von jdm. — **at times** bisweilen — **harsh** streng — **to discipline s.o.** ('dɪsəplɪn) jdn. disziplinieren — **Jim Crow laws** zwischen Ende des 19. Jhdts. und Mitte des 20. Jhdts. in den US-Südstaaten geltende Gesetze zur Rassentrennung

9   **to push s.o. toward s.th.** h.: jdn. zu etw. bewegen — **deputy** stellvertretende(r) — **fearful;** s.w.u. **apprehensive** (,æprɪ'hensɪv) ängstlich — **to do one's part** seinen Teil beitragen — **to model** h.: zeigen — **ethical** ethisch — **accountable** (ə'kaʊntəbəl) verantwortungsbewusst; s.w.u. **to hold s.o. a.** jdn. zur Verantwortung ziehen — **compassionate** (kəm'pæʃənət) Anteil nehmend

10   **misconduct** (,mɪs'kɒndʌkt) Fehlverhalten; s.w.u. **conduct** Verhalten — **administratively** (əd'mɪnɪstrətɪvli) administrativ — **to intervene** (,ɪntə'viːn) eingreifen — **to take on** h.: übernehmen — **perception** Sichtweise

11   **to forge s.th.** (fɔːdʒ) etw. schmieden; h.: etw. aufbauen — **delicate navigation** behutsames Vorgehen — **traitor; sellout** Verräter — **Uncle Tom** abfällige Bezeichnung für vermeintliche Verräter der afroamerikanischen Gemeinschaft — **to come to mind** in den Sinn kommen — **to understand where s.o. is coming from** jds. Standpunkt nachvollziehen können — **to rethink s.th.** etw. überdenken

10 Officers involved in misconduct should be held accountable criminally or administratively, he said, and rules should require their colleagues to intervene if they witness unethical conduct and to report bad behavior. Boatwright also said it's important for his colleagues in the department to understand why Black people might be apprehensive or respond negatively during interactions with police. He's been taking on those conversations. "I try to let them know that although that person may have a perception, that perception is a reality, that feeling is real," Boatwright said.

11 For Black police officers, forging relationships in their own community requires delicate navigation. Some say they have been called a race traitor, sellout, or Uncle Tom while in uniform. "When I receive that myself, being a Black man, yeah, the first thing that comes to mind, I'm hurt. But then I try to understand where they are coming from," Boatwright said, adding that it never made him rethink his career choice. "I still think there's a job I can do." …

'Defund the Police'

POLICING
What it means depends on who you ask, writes John Wisely.

1 PROTESTERS in Detroit and elsewhere say they have a good way to rein in police misconduct: Defund the police. So what does that mean? Reduce police budgets? Eliminate them entirely? Consolidate or disband outright whole police departments?

2 No one has offered a specific proposal, but Tristan Taylor, one of the leaders of the Detroit protests, has said he wants Detroit Police to get rid of military-style equipment and have the city shift money out of the police budget into things such as conflict resolution, housing, and other needs.

3 New York City Mayor Bill de Blasio announced last week that he would reduce the budget of the New York Police Department and shift money into youth and social services. He didn't specify how much of the department's $6 billion budget would be shifted, saying only that it would be worked out in the budget process. The City Council in Minneapolis wants to go further and disband that city's police department in response to the death of George Floyd.

4 The International Association of Chiefs of Police slammed the idea of defunding. "This is a misguided, shortsighted approach to achieving the change that we all seek," the group said in a statement. "All that defunding and shifting resources away from the police will accomplish is to further reduce the ability of police leaders to enact the positive change that is required."

5 Local police agree. "I think investing in social programs, whether it's programs for our youth, programs that take police officers away from nonviolent issues involving the mentally ill, that makes sense," Detroit Police Chief James Craig said in an interview with Fox2 Detroit. "But you don't take it away from police." Craig said that Detroit defunded the police when it went through bankruptcy, cutting officer pay 10%. Morale among police officers tanked, and the Police Department struggled, he said. …

6 It typically takes a severe economic downturn before community leaders cut police budgets, said Jeremy Wilson, a professor of criminal justice at Michigan State University, who studies police department consolidations. "Public safety has typically been that sacred institution that isn't touched," Wilson said. "But when things become kind of a crisis due to economics, questions start coming up like, OK we've got to make such fundamental cuts. The vast majority of police budgets are staffing, and the vast majority of community budgets are police."

7 Wilson said that's when some cities will consider merging with other departments or contracting for police service from a nearby local government, often a county sheriff. Money savings is typically the main reason for the change, but police performance is sometimes a factor as well. Wilson said that was the case in one community he studied, ⟳

0–1 **TO DEFUND S.TH.** etw. die Finanzierung entziehen — **policing** Polizeiarbeit — **to rein in** (reɪn) in den Griff bekommen — **misconduct** (ˌmɪsˈkɒndʌkt) Fehlverhalten — **to eliminate** abschaffen — **to consolidate** (kənˈsɒlɪdeɪt) zus. legen; s.w.u. **consolidation** Zus.legung — **to disband** auflösen — **outright** vollständig

2–3 **to have s.o. do s.th.** möchten, dass jd. etw. tut — **to shift** umverteilen — **conflict resolution** Konfliktbewältigung — **housing** Wohnraum — **billion** Milliarde — **to work s.th. out** etw. ausarbeiten — **budget process** Haushaltsverfahren

4 **to slam** scharf kritisieren — **misguided** (ˌmɪsˈgaɪdɪd) verfehlt — **shortsighted** kurzsichtig — **to seek s.th.** etw. anstreben — **to accomplish** (əˈkʌmplɪʃ) erreichen — **to enact** h.: bewirken

5–6 **nonviolent** (ˌ-ˈvaɪələnt) nicht gewalttätig — **the mentally ill** Personen mit psychischer Erkrankung — **bankruptcy** (ˈbæŋkrəptsi) Insolvenz — **morale** (məˈrɑːl) Moral — **to tank** (fig) einbrechen — **to take** h.: brauchen — **economic downturn** Konjunkturabschwung — **criminal justice** Strafjustiz — **sacred** (ˈseɪkrɪd) heilig; ehrwürdig — **cuts** h.: (fig) Einschnitte — **staffing** Personal

7–8 **to merge** (mɜːdʒ) s. zus.schließen — **to contract** e-n Vertrag abschließen — **money savings** Kosteneinsparungen —

⊃ Compton, California, which disbanded its police force in 2000.

8 "I think a lot of it had to do with the kind of policing of the city," he said. "It kind of lost favor with the community and so they disbanded the police department and brought in the L.A. sheriff." In that instance, the change led to improved policing, Wilson said. "After the L.A. sheriff came in, our analysis showed that there were statistically significant increases in clearance rate and that there was a reduction in burglary," he said. "We kind of attributed that to the fact that the L.A. sheriff had more resources and had a greater kind of professionalism and capacity."

9 Wilson said that case can provide lessons for others, but they are not universal. "The thing to be careful about here is that all these different forms of consolidation are often kind of considered a silver bullet in some ways," he said. "But what my work has shown is there are no silver bullets here. Everything is context specific. And so what works well in one community may or may not work well in another. It depends on the political will, the community will, resources, existing infrastructure. There's a whole host of factors."

10 William King is a professor of criminal justice at Boise State University whose specialty is disbanded police departments. He has researched dozens of departments that have closed for various reasons. "In my interviews, everybody mentions budgets, that it was a budget issue and they saved money," he said. "But in about a third of the places, there were other things. The police department had misconduct; sometimes the cops were engaging in crime. The cops didn't get along with the local politicians. There were just serious disagreements about how policing should be done." …

11 The concept of counties taking over for cities has been tried in metro Detroit. In the late 2000s, the City of Pontiac was heavily in debt. Its police department, which once had 220 officers, had been cut down to 50. Response times for many 911 calls were 80 minutes. The city disbanded its department and signed a contract with the Oakland County Sheriff's Office to provide service. The sheriff hired most of the Pontiac officers and added to their ranks, bringing a total of 74 deputies to Pontiac.

12 Because most of the command staffers were already in place at the sheriff's headquarters, the department was able to put more deputies on the street, Sheriff Michael Bouchard said. "There were some very good police officers there, but they were working in a system that didn't allow them

A protester *in Brooklyn.* | PHOTO: *Getty Images*

to succeed on many levels," Bouchard said. Since the change, violent crime is down 40% and response times on priority calls is about six minutes, Bouchard said.

13 Macomb County Sheriff Tony Wickersham said defunding police would make it harder to keep up with the times. Policing has changed over the years. Even the deputies themselves have changed. Younger deputies today are more conscious of work-life balance and don't immediately jump at the chance to work overtime, he said.

14 Wickersham said a good reform that could come from the current debate would be to create uniform training standards across the country with federal money to pay for it. That way, no department would be using outdated methods because they couldn't afford to learn better ones.

---

to lose favor with s.o. ('feɪvə) jds. Gunst verlieren — **in that instance** in diesem Fall — **clearance rate** ('klɪərəns) Aufklärungsquote — **to attribute s.th. to s.th.** (ə'trɪbjuːt) etw. auf etw. zurückführen — **professionalism** (prə'feʃənəlɪzəm) Professionalität

9–10 to be considered s.th. (kən'sɪdəd) als etw. angesehen werden — **silver bullet** ('bʊlɪt) Patentlösung — **context specific** kontextspezifisch — **a whole host of** e-e ganze Reihe von — **specialty** ('speʃəlti) Fachgebiet — **dozens** ('dʌzənz) Dutzende — **to engage in crime** in Verbrechen verwickelt sein — **to get along with s.o.** mit jdm. auskommen

11–12 metro Detroit die Metropolregion D. — **heavily in debt** (det) hoch verschuldet — **response time** Reaktionszeit — **911 call** Notruf — **ranks** h.: Belegschaft — **deputy** ('depjəti) Polizeibeamter(-in) — **command staffers** leitende Mitarbeiter — **to be in place** vorhanden sein — **to allow s.o. to do s.th.** jdm. ermöglichen, etw. zu tun — **priority call** dringender Anruf

13–14 to keep up with the times mit der Zeit Schritt halten — **work-life balance** Ausgleich zwischen Berufs- und Privatleben — **to jump at s.th.** s. um etw. reißen — **uniform** ('juːnɪfɔːm) einheitlich — **federal money** Bundesgelder

For Years, California Police Agencies Have Rejected Almost Every Racial Profiling Complaint They Received

RACIAL PROFILING From 2016 to 2019, police agencies across California upheld less than 2% of the roughly 3,500 profiling complaints filed, write James Queally and Ben Poston.

1 THE MORE time attorney Chris Martin spent in handcuffs on a February night in South L.A. earlier this year, the more it became obvious to him why he was being detained. Martin – the 32-year-old director of legal services for Black Lives Matter Los Angeles – was driving to a mentoring program when he came upon what he described as a "police perimeter." He asked if he could go through. Instead, he said, officers asked him to exit his vehicle.

2 Within minutes, Martin said, he was frisked and handcuffed. The officers said they were looking for a shooting suspect described only as a "Black man in dark clothing." They offered no further reason for the stop, Martin said. Eventually, Martin was released. He filed a complaint alleging officers detained him only because he was Black. But he already knew how the investigation would end. "I still have to file the complaint, even though I know that it's highly likely to be futile, at least as far as whether or not the department is going to hold itself accountable," he said. "We know that they won't."

3 Police agencies across the state upheld just 49 racial profiling complaints from 2016 to 2019, less than 2% of the roughly 3,500 allegations filed, a *Los Angeles Times* analysis of California Department of Justice statistics found. Of the 250 law enforcement agencies that received at least one racial profiling complaint in that time frame, 92% of them upheld none of them, according to the analysis.

4 The Los Angeles County Sheriff's Department sustained two out of 146 complaints in the same time span, according to the analysis. Despite receiving 883 racial profiling complaints during that four-year period, the most in the state, the Los Angeles Police Department upheld only two.

5 Police agencies in California have a long history of rejecting allegations of officer misconduct. A prior *Times* analysis found that from 2008 to 2017, police throughout the state upheld only 8% of roughly 200,000 allegations of wrongdoing they had received from the public. …

6 Walter Katz, former independent auditor of the San Jose Police Department, said that despite numerous reports that have highlighted racial bias in police stops and searches, proving an individual contact between an officer and a civilian is racially biased can be extremely challenging. That divide often infuriates those who file complaints, who inevitably see an officer's version of events validated over their own.

7 "You know the undercurrent of what is occurring is discriminatory, but being able to prove that is different," said Katz, who is now vice president of criminal justice policy for Arnold Ventures. "Really, in the absence of a statement by the officer or deputy proving racial animus, proving such complaints is really difficult."

8 This year, a report from the LAPD's inspector general found Black and Latino drivers were far more likely to be stopped by police than white mo- ⮞

0–1 **AGENCY** h.: Behörde — **to uphold;** s.w.u. **to sustain** (sə'steɪn) stattgeben — **to file** einreichen — **attorney** Anwalt/Anwältin — **handcuffs** ('-kʌfs) Handschellen; s.w.u. **to handcuff s.o.** jdm. Handschellen anlegen — **to detain s.o.** jdn. festhalten — **mentoring program** Mentorenprogramm — **to come upon s.th.** auf etw. stoßen — **perimeter** (pə'rɪmɪtə) h.: Absperrung

2–4 **to frisk s.o.** jdn. durchsuchen — **to allege** (ə'ledʒ) vorwerfen; s.w.u. **allegation** (ˌælə'geɪʃən) Vorwurf — **futile** ('fjuːtaɪl) aussichtslos — **to hold s.o. accountable** (ə'kaʊntəbəl) jdn. zur Verantwortung ziehen — **state** h.: US-Bundesstaat — **Department of Justice** Justizministerium — **law enforcement** (ɪn'fɔːsmənt) Polizei- — **time frame;** s.w.u. **time span** Zeitraum

5 **history** h.: Vorgeschichte — **misconduct** (ˌ-'kɒndʌkt); s.w.u. **wrongdoing** Fehlverhalten — **prior** ('praɪə) vorherig — **throughout the state** im gesamten Bundesstaat

6 **auditor** ('ɔːdɪtə) Prüfer(in) — **numerous** ('njuːmərəs) zahlreich — **bias** ('baɪəs) Vorurteil; s.w.u. **to be biased** Vorurteile haben — **police stops and searches** polizeiliche Kontrollen und Durchsuchungen — **civilian** Zivilist(in) — **divide;** s.w.u. **chasm** ('kæzəm) Kluft — **to infuriate s.o.** (ɪn'fjʊərɪeɪt) jdn. erzürnen — **inevitably** (ɪ'nevɪtəbli) unweigerlich — **to validate** ('vælɪdeɪt) h.: als erwiesen ansehen

7–9 **undercurrent** ('--ˌkʌrənt) (fig) Unterton — **criminal justice policy** Strafjustizpolitik — **in the absence of** ('æbsəns) in Ermangelung von — **deputy (sheriff)** h.: Polizeibeamter(-in) (d. stellvertretend) — **animus** ('ænɪməs) Feindseligkeit; Gesinnung — **inspector general** Generalinspekteur(in) —

torists, though white drivers were more likely to have contraband when searched. A 2016 Stanford University study also found that 60% of the people stopped by Oakland police in a one-year period were Black, even though just 28% of the city's population was Black at the time.

9   Although he understands why the numbers might concern some, LeRonne Armstrong, a deputy chief in the Oakland Police Department, said his agency thoroughly reviews each profiling complaint. If an allegation of racial bias is made in the field, he said, a supervisor is immediately dispatched to the scene.

10   Armstrong said footage from body-worn cameras often disproves allegations of racial profiling. But he understood why diminished trust between the public and police might put a chasm between what a person believes and what an internal investigation can substantiate. "It's so hard sometimes, to prove what people feel," he said. "Not to say that their feeling is wrong, or what they perceive is completely off base, but it's just sometimes very challenging when you have investigative standards that you need to reach to hold somebody accountable."

11   But asking the public to simply trust the validity of internal investigations can be a hard sell, experts say. California law shields virtually all information about internal affairs allegations from public view, except when the allegation concerns lying, sexual assault, or use of force ending in death or serious harm. Those who make racial profiling complaints, however, will receive only a form letter noting that their complaint was upheld or rejected.

12   Priscilla Ocen, a member of the L.A. County Sheriff Civilian Oversight Commission, said that one-way flow of information leaves people who make profiling and misconduct allegations feeling as if they were not heard. Statistics such as those revealed in *The Times'* analysis only cement the impression that police will not police themselves, she said. "This is the problem that we have, where there's an implicit trust and belief in whatever the officers' account is," she said. "The complainants' account is the one that is being subject to scrutiny. I think that's really the problem. There's an inherent power imbalance in these investigations. The deputy's word is almost always taken at face value." …

13   Although the standards for sustaining racial profiling complaints might make it difficult for police agencies to uphold more complaints, Katz said agencies can do more to make residents feel as if their allegations aren't simply being [thrown out]. A number of police agencies, including the LAPD, use mediation programs in which an accuser and officers can discuss the conduct in question outside the confines of an internal investigation or disciplinary process.

14   Otherwise, Katz said, the gap between statistical evidence of systemic bias in policing and the lack of action on individual cases will only continue to harm the public's trust in law enforcement. "I think that the evidence is clear and ample research backs this up. There is evidence of racial bias and discriminatory policing," he said. "The challenge is how does one connect together what is evidence of systemic bias, down to the individual officer level. Two different standards are being applied."

---

contraband Schmuggelware — **to concern s.o.** jdn. beunruhigen — **to review** prüfen — **in the field** vor Ort — **supervisor** Dienstvorgesetzte(r) — **to dispatch** entsenden

10   **footage** ('fʊtɪdʒ) Aufnahmen — **body-worn camera** am Körper getragene Kamera — **to disprove s.th.** (dɪ'spruːv) etw. widerlegen — **diminished** (dɪ'mɪnɪʃt) vermindert — **to substantiate** (səb'stænʃieɪt) belegen — **not so say that …** was nicht heißen soll, dass … — **to perceive** (pə'siːv) wahrnehmen — **to be off base** falschliegen — **investigative standards** (ɪn'vestɪɡətɪv) Untersuchungsstandards

11   **validity** (və'lɪdəti) Richtigkeit — **to be a hard sell** (fig) schwer verständlich zu machen — **to shield s.th. from public view** (ʃiːld) etw. vor der Öffentlichkeit verbergen — **internal affairs** innere Angelegenheiten — **sexual assault** (ə'sɒlt) sexueller Übergriff — **form letter** Formbrief

12   **civilian oversight** (sɪ'vɪljən) zivile Kontrolle — **one-way flow of information** einseitiger Informationsfluss — **to cement** zementieren — **to police** (polizeilich) kontrollieren; s.w.u. **policing** Polizeiarbeit — **implicit** (ɪm'plɪsɪt) bedingungslos — **complainant** (kəm'pleɪnənt); s.w.u. **accuser** (ə'kjuːzə) Beschwerdeführer(in) — **to be subject to scrutiny** ('skruːtɪni) auf dem Prüfstand stehen — **inherent** (ɪn'herənt) innewohnend — **power imbalance** Machtgefälle — **to take s.th. at face value** etw. für bare Münze nehmen

13-14 **mediation program** Mediationsprogramm — **the conduct in question** das fragliche Verhalten — **outside the confines of s.th.** ('kɒnfaɪnz) unabhängig von etw. (**confines** Grenzen) — **disciplinary process** (ˌdɪsə'plɪnəri) Disziplinarverfahren — **ample** reichlich — **to back up** h.: bestätigen

Early Police Stops Have Long-Term Criminal Justice Consequences for Black Youth

POLICE ENCOUNTERS
According to a study, police stops during childhood increase the risk of arrests in young adulthood for Black students but not white students, write Elise Takahama et al.

1   ANNIE MCGLYNN-WRIGHT could find no shortage of painful examples of police stopping Black youth when she was working through her University of Washington research – but she wanted to learn more about what happened after those stops and how those early-in-life experiences, depending on race, might shape the rest of a child's life.

2   The results of the UW study, which was published in late October, were straightforward: Police encounters during childhood increase the risk of arrests in young adulthood for Black students but not white students.

3   The study, launched nearly 20 years ago, comes in the midst of a national reckoning on racial justice and after months of protests following the police killing of George Floyd in Minneapolis. The study "just kind of reinforces much of what we've been focused on in the last eight months after the tragic death of George Floyd," said Kevin Haggerty, a professor in UW's School of Social Work and a co-author of the research. "And it really brings that to light in a very real way."

4   While past research on race and policing has shown evidence Black Americans experience more frequent police stops and are more likely to have a negative experience during those stops, UW researchers noticed there wasn't as much information about the long-term consequences of those early experiences with law enforcement, said McGlynn-Wright, a postdoctoral fellow at Tulane University who led the study while pursuing her doctorate at UW. "There was some sense that early contacts might matter … but (no studies) that we were aware of how that might be different by race," McGlynn-Wright said.

5   The study tracked 331 Black and white Seattle Public Schools (SPS) students who were eighth graders at 18 different schools in 2001 and 2002. Researchers interviewed students and parents when the kids were about 13 years old, surveyed them several times over the years, then interviewed them again when they were 20. The UW team wanted to examine what happens during the first few police stops of a young person's life, and how – depending on race – they might affect how that person is treated when they transition into young adulthood.

6   The study found that while there were no differences in illegal behavior between Black and white students in eighth grade, 37% of Black teens said they had had some sort of contact with police, compared with 22% of white teens. And by the time the students had turned 20, 53% of white participants reported engaging in some level of criminal behavior, compared with 32% of Black participants. While white participants were more likely to report illegal drug use, there weren't any significant differences by race for violent or property crimes, the study showed.

7   One of the main and most alarming takeaways, McGlynn-Wright said, was that despite the fact that whites reported higher rates of illegal behavior at age 20, Black youth who had had contact with police were 11 times more likely to have been arrested by age 20 than their Black peers who had not had that first contact with police. On the other hand, early police contacts didn't appear to matter in later outcomes for white youth.

8   "Even when police act politely, highly discretionary stops send messages about assumed criminality and citizenship," the study said. "Racially biased investigatory stops tell a driver that they look like a criminal and people like them are subject to arbitrary control befitting their subordinate status." ⟲

0–2   **POLICE STOP** Polizeikontrolle — **criminal justice consequences** (kɒnsɪkwənsɪz) strafrechtliche Konsequenzen — **encounter** Begegnung — **adulthood** ('ædʌlthʊd) Erwachsenenalter — **et al** und andere — **to work through s.th.** etw. durcharbeiten — **early-in-life** in jungen Jahren — **to shape s.o./s.th.** (fig) jdn./etw. prägen

3–4   **in the midst of** (mɪdst) vor dem Hintergrund — **reckoning** Aufarbeitung — **to reinforce** (,riːɪnˈfɔːs) bekräftigen — **social work** Sozialarbeit; s.w.u. **social services** Sozialdienste — **co-author** Mitautor(in) — **to bring s.th. to light** (fig) etw. ans Licht bringen — **policing** Polizeiarbeit — **law enforcement** (ɪnˈfɔːsmənt) Polizei — **postdoctoral fellow** (,-ˈdɒktərəl) Postdoktorand(in) — **to pursue s.th.** (pəˈsjuː) etw. anstreben — **doctorate** ('dɒktərət) Doktortitel

5–7   **to track** (nach)verfolgen; h.: begleiten — **eighth grader** Achtklässler(in) — **to survey** (-'-) befragen — **to transition into s.th.** in etw. übergehen — **by the time** als — **participant** (paːˈtɪsɪpənt) Teilnehmer(in) — **to engage in s.th.** h.: etw. an den Tag legen — **violent or property crimes** Gewalt- oder Eigentumsdelikte — **take-away** Schlussfolgerung — **peer** Gleichaltrige(r) — **outcome** Auswirkung; Folge

8   **highly** hochgradig — **discretionary** (dɪˈskreʃənəri); s.w.u. **arbitrary** ('ɑːbɪtrəri) willkürlich —

9 The study also looked at the introduction of resource officers in schools, which has increased opportunities for contact between police and children and, according to the study, is "frequently attributed to a rise in public concern about school violence." "Limiting the contact police have with young people is a really important first step," McGlynn-Wright said.

10 While McGlynn-Wright acknowledged SPS resource officers could be seen as counselor or mentor figures for students, she added that "there's a legally ambiguous area that they enter into where it's not entirely clear if they're acting as a school personnel or a police officer."

11 The study's results reemphasize the importance of focusing police officers' attention on the quality of their interactions with young people, Haggerty added. "It may be that law enforcement personnel or public safety personnel are not the people who should be doing counseling in schools," he said. "There are other folks who have that role."

12 Seattle police Chief Adrian Diaz said recently the Police Department didn't have a formal school resource officer program in 2001 or 2002, when the survey began. The partnership between the department and SPS began in 2008. (The research, while studying Seattle students, is not specifically about stops or contact with the Seattle Police Department.)

13 "All the programs we've built since then have focused on making sure we're not contributing to the school-to-prison pipeline. ... We're not part of that disciplinary process," Diaz said. He added that officers, whose goal is to act as role models to students, were not making arrests in schools and have done "hundreds of thousands of referrals into social services."

14 There's still a lot that researchers don't know about how and why police stops have much longer-term consequences for Black youth. And while the report didn't specifically examine the reasoning behind the disparities, the authors' research points to the effects of "stereotypes of Black criminality," McGlynn-Wright said. "Police start to respond to them more as if they're criminals," she said. "And for white kids it's like, 'Oh, the kid just did something wrong.'" ...

---

assumed (ə'sjuːmd) vermutet — **criminality** Kriminalität — **citizenship** Staatsangehörigkeit — **racially biased** ('baɪəst) auf ethnischen Vorurteilen basierend — **investigatory** (ɪnˈvestɪgətəri) Ermittlungs- — **to be subject to s.th.** etw. ausgesetzt sein — **befitting s.o./s.th.** jdm./etw. zukommend — **subordinate** (səˈbɔːdɪnət) untergeordnet
9–11 resource officer Einsatzbeamte(r) — **to attribute s.th. to s.th.** (əˈtrɪbjuːt) e-e S. auf etw. zurückführen — **to acknowledge** (əkˈnɒlɪdʒ) (fig) einräumen — **counselor** ('kaʊnsələ) Berater(in); s.w.u. **counseling** Beratung — **ambiguous** (æmˈbɪgjuəs) h.: unklar — **to enter into s.th.** h.: s. in etw. begeben — **personnel** Personal — **to reemphasize** (ˌriːˈemfəsaɪz) erneut betonen
12–14 formal offiziell — **to build** h.: einrichten — **school-to-prison pipeline** Schule-Gefängnis-Pipeline — **disciplinary** (ˌdɪsəˈplɪnəri) disziplinarisch — **role model** Vorbild — **referral** (rɪˈfɜːrəl) h.: Weiterleitung — **reasoning** h.: Gründe — **disparity** Diskrepanz — **to point to s.th.** (fig) auf etw. hindeuten

---

The Proud History of Black Protest in Sport

ACTIVISM IN SPORT Sportsmen and women have always been at the forefront of the fight for civil rights, write Peter Olusoga and David Olusoga.

1 WE MAY never know why Jake Hepple, a now unemployed welder from Burnley, thought it was a good idea to hire a plane and have it trail a banner reading "White Lives Matter Burnley" across the skies over Manchester's Etihad Stadium. What we are assured is that Hepple was not motivated by any form of racism. After all, he told reporters: "I've got lots of black and Asian friends."

2 The phrase "White Lives Matter" is, of course, an attack on the phrase "Black Lives Matter" and the movement that coalesced around it. But while one is a plea for equality, the other, along with the phrase "All Lives Matter", was created by those who engage in the pantomime of pretending that anyone is suggesting only black lives matter. These people belong to the same demographic as those who think structural racism doesn't exist or that black people should "get over" slavery.

3 The light plane that Hepple hired to pull his banner was timed to appear over the stadium just after kick-off and not long after the players had taken a knee in memory of George Floyd. The Burnley players, along with their opponents were, like players across the Premier League, also wearing Black Lives Matter badges.

4 The wearing of BLM badges on playing shirts was proposed by captains from various clubs and highlights how footballers increasingly use their platform to bring attention to social issues. Raheem Sterling has been vocal about media treat-

An image *of Manchester United's striker Marcus Rashford is pictured alongside a message of thanks to him for his campaign to get Britain's government to extend the free school meals for children during the COVID-19 pandemic.* | PHOTO: *Getty Images*

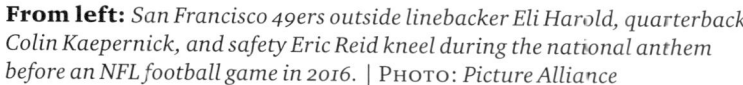

From left: *San Francisco 49ers outside linebacker Eli Harold, quarterback Colin Kaepernick, and safety Eric Reid kneel during the national anthem before an NFL football game in 2016.* | PHOTO: *Picture Alliance*

ment of black players and the lack of non-white coaches and managers in the sport. His England teammate Marcus Rashford recently forced the government into a spectacular U-turn on the issue of free school meals. In a league in which about a third of players are not white, taking the knee was as much an act of solidarity as of political protest.

5 Kneeling like this was first popularised in the US in 2016 by the NFL quarterback Colin Kaepernick. Kaepernick began his protest against systemic racism and police brutality by sitting on the bench rather than standing during the pre-game rendition of "The Star-Spangled Banner" when he played for the San Francisco 49ers. It was Nate Boyer, a Special Forces veteran and an ex-NFL player, who suggested that taking a knee was a more respectful but equally powerful protest. This silent, peaceful gesture became a symbol of the Black Lives Matter movement.

6 Kaepernick's career, and his chance to etch his name into the NFL's record books, was taken from him. In response to his protest, the owners of the 32 NFL teams effectively colluded to keep him and his teammate Eric Reid out of the league. Almost all those owners are white, and some are Donald Trump supporters and Republican party donors. The US president's reaction to Kaepernick's protest was as crude as it was predictable. Speaking at a Republican campaign rally in 2017, he said: "Wouldn't you love to see one of these NFL owners, when somebody disrespects our flag, to say: 'Get that son of a bitch off the field right now, out. He's fired. He's fired!'"

7 But Kaepernick was not alone. Months before Trump's attack on Kaepernick, players in the US Women's National Basketball Association (WNBA), including Maya Moore, had begun their own protest after the deaths of Philando Castile and Alton Sterling. Moore, who some regard as the greatest WNBA player of all time, has since taken two full seasons away from the game, in part to focus on social justice. ⮞

⁰⁻¹ **TO BE AT the forefront** an vorderster Front stehen — **civil rights** Bürgerrechte — **welder** Schweißer(in) — **to trail** h.: hinter s. herziehen — **banner** Schleppbanner — **reading** h.: mit der Beschriftung — **motivated** motiviert
² **movement** Bewegung — **to coalesce** (kəʊə'les) s. formieren — **plea** (pli:) Plädoyer — **to engage in s.th.** s. an etw. beteiligen — **pantomime** ('pæntəmaɪm) (fig) Posse — **demographic** demografische Gruppe — **structural racism** ('strʌktʃərəl); s.w.u. **systemic r.** institutioneller Rassismus — **slavery** Sklaverei
³⁻⁴ **light plane** Leichtflugzeug — **to time** zeitlich abstimmen — **kick-off** Anpfiff — **to take a knee** Protestgeste, bei der s. die Spieler hinknien — **in memory of** in Erinnerung an — **to be vocal** ('vəʊkəl) s. lautstark äußern — **teammate** Teamkollege(-in) — **U-turn** Kehrtwende — **school meals** Schulessen
⁵ **to popularise s.th.** ('pɒpjələraɪz) etw. populär machen — **police brutality** polizeiliche Übergriffe — **pre-game; s.w.u. pre-match** vor dem Spiel — **rendition** Darbietung — **The Star-Spangled Banner** ('stɑːspæŋɡəld); s.w.u. **US national anthem** ('ænθəm) US-Nationalhymne — **respectful** respektvoll; s.w.u. **to disrespect** (,--'-) nicht respektieren — **gesture** ('dʒestʃə) Geste
⁶ **to etch** ätzen; h.: s. verewigen — **to take s.th. from s.o.** jdm. etw. nehmen — **effectively** h.: im Grunde — **to collude** (kə'luːd) s. verschwören — **donor** ('dəʊnə) Spender(in); Geldgeber(in) — **crude** (kruːd) vulgär — **predictable** (prɪ'dɪktəbəl) vorhersehbar — **campaign rally** Wahlkampfveranstaltung — **son of a bitch** (vulgar) Hurensohn
⁷⁻⁸ **of all time** aller Zeiten — **to take (time) away from s.th.** s. von etw. zurückziehen — **in part** teilweise —

↻ **8** And 20 years before Kaepernick and Moore there was the basketball player Mahmoud Abdul-Rauf. The fact that his name sparks so little recognition today demonstrates how effectively his career was wrecked after he too engaged in political protest. In the early 90s, Abdul-Rauf was well on his way to becoming one of the NBA's top players. But in 1996, he refused to stand for the pre-match singing of the US national anthem. He was fined and suspended from the league for 12 games. …

9 Today, Trump and others feel the need to condemn players such as Kaepernick and Moore because star athletes have reach. The NBA basketball star LeBron James is one of the most recognisable athletes on the planet – with 46.5 million Twitter followers. In Britain, Manchester United's Marcus Rashford has 3 million, a comparatively modest number but considerably more than the foreign secretary, Dominic Raab, who last month said that taking the knee "seems to be taken from the Game of Thrones". …

10 Ever since the Black Lives Matter protests began to spread across the world, commentators have drawn comparisons between 2020 and 1968, the year Martin Luther King was assassinated and riots and protests tore across the US. Then, as now, sport was not a distraction from politics and the demands for civil rights but one of the engines driving them forward.

11 In 1968, Muhammad Ali was not, in the minds of millions of white Americans, a sporting legend but a pariah. The previous year he had refused to be inducted into the US army, then at war in Vietnam. For this, he was sentenced to five years in prison (which he did not serve), stripped of his passport, and refused a boxing licence in every US state. Ali in 1968 was the embodiment of black political radicalism, but it was Tommie Smith and John Carlos, two US sprinters at the 1968 Mexico Olympic Games, who provided the civil rights movement with its most iconic image.

12 Smith and Carlos won gold and bronze in the 200m. During the medal ceremony, as "The Star-Spangled Banner" played, they stood on the podium, shoeless to represent African-American poverty, beads around their necks to protest against lynchings, heads bowed, and black-gloved fists raised skywards as symbols of black power and unity. That black power fist appears on the Black Lives Matter badges currently being worn by Premier League players.

Tommie Smith *(1st place) and John Carlos (3rd place) of the US raise their fists in the "Black Power Salute" during the playing of the national anthem at the Olympics in Mexico City in 1968.* | PHOTO: *Getty Images*

13 While the parallels between 1968 and 2020 are clear, what is happening now does feel different. In the US, the NFL that ended Kaepernick's playing career has, in 2020, backed down and will allow players to kneel during the anthem in the upcoming season.

14 A cynic would say that these are institutions that can feel the shift in public opinion and are simply making shrewd business decisions. The hope has to be that, unlike Smith, Carlos, and Ali in 1968 and Kaepernick in 2016, black sportsmen such as Rashford and Sterling will be supported and celebrated rather than vilified for using their voices to fight for social change.

© 2020 Guardian News and Media Ltd

---

to spark zünden; h.: hervorrufen — **recognition** (ˌrekəgˈnɪʃən) Beachtung — **to wreck** (rek) ruinieren — **to be well on one's way** auf dem besten Weg sein
9   **to feel the need to do s.th.** das Bedürfnis verspüren, etw. zu tun — **to condemn s.o.** (kənˈdem) (fig) jdn. verurteilen — **reach** Reichweite; Einfluss — **recognisable** (ˈrekəgnaɪzəbəl) bekannt — **comparatively** (kəmˈpærətɪvli) vergleichsweise — **foreign secretary** Außenminister(in)
10   **to draw comparisons** (kəmˈpærɪsənz) Vergleiche ziehen — **to assassinate** (əˈsæsɪneɪt) ermorden — **riots** (ˈraɪəts) Unruhen — **to tear** h.: wüten — **distraction** Ablenkung — **engine** h.: (fig) treibende Kraft — **to drive s.th. forward** (fig) etw. vorantreiben
11   **in s.o.'s minds** (fig) in jds. Augen — **pariah** (pəˈraɪə) Aussätzige(r) — **to induct** (ɪnˈdʌkt) (in die Armee) einziehen — **to serve** h.: verbüßen — **to strip s.o. of s.th.** jdm. etw. entziehen — **embodiment** Verkörperung; Inbegriff — **sprinter** Kurzstreckenläufer(in) — **iconic** (aɪˈkɒnɪk) mit Symbolcharakter
12   **podium** Siegerpodest — **shoeless** ohne Schuhe — **beads** Perlen; h.: Kette — **lynching** (ˈlɪntʃɪŋ) Lynchmord — **bowed** (baʊd) gesenkt — **fist** Faust — **skywards** (ˈskaɪwəds) himmelwärts — **unity** Einigkeit
13–14 to back down nachgeben — **upcoming** bevorstehend — **cynic** (ˈsɪnɪk) Zyniker(in) — **shift** Wandel — **shrewd** (ʃruːd) clever — **to vilify s.o.** (ˈvɪlɪfaɪ) jdn. verunglimpfen — **to use one's voice** (fig) seine Stimme (für etw.) einsetzen

'We Are Scared as Black People in America'

LEBRON JAMES The Los Angeles Lakers player tells Mark Medina what reforms need to happen so that police are held accountable when they kill unarmed Black people.

LeBron James *of the Los Angeles Lakers.*
| PHOTO: *Getty Images*

1 THE LANGUAGE and tone fully captured LeBron James' ongoing frustration with police killing unarmed Black people. "It's just (expletive) up in our community," James said. "I know people get tired of hearing me say it. But we are scared as Black people in America. Black men, Black women, Black kids, we are terrified."

2 With horror, James watched footage that showed police officers shooting Jacob Blake, an unarmed Black man in Kenosha, Wisconsin, seven times. James expressed gratitude "through the grace of God that he's still living" and offered support and prayers toward the Blake family. James also expressed frustration with yet another incident of police brutality toward unarmed Black people.

3 "If you're sitting here and telling me that there was no way to subdue that gentleman or detain him just before the firing of guns, then you're sitting here and lying to not only me," James said.

"But you're lying to every African American, every Black person in the community, because we see it over and over and over."

4 They saw it in 2013 when George Zimmerman shot 17-year-old Trayvon Martin despite being unarmed and wearing a hoodie in his Florida neighborhood. They saw it in 2014 when a police officer choked and killed Eric Garner. They saw it in March when three police officers mistook Breonna Taylor as a suspect for an ex-boyfriend's laundering operation and killed her while she was asleep. They saw it on Memorial Day weekend when a police officer knelt and killed George Floyd. And they saw it on Sunday when Kenosha police responded to a domestic incident by shooting Blake seven times as he was walking unarmed toward his car.

5 "There were multiple moments where if they wanted to, they could've tackled him. They could've grabbed him," James said. "They could've done that. Why does it always have to get to a point where we see the guns firing, and his family is there, and the kids are there. It's in broad daylight. If that video is not being taken by that person across the street, do we even know if we even see that video?"

6 James sounded annoyed, exasperated, and tired as he spoke for nearly 15 minutes following the Lakers' win over the Portland Trail Blazers on Monday. He had wanted to honor former Lakers legend Kobe Bryant as the team honored what would have been his 42nd birthday Sunday if not for his passing seven months ago. But no. "I can't ever enjoy a playoff win right now, which is the sad part." James said.

7 Another sad part? James had spoken at length about this topic already for the past four months. He became among the first athletes to speak out about Floyd's killing. He had devoted several post-game press conferences calling for police to be held accountable for Taylor's killing. And on Monday, James detailed how Blake's shooting captures why many in the Black community distrust law enforcement. ➲

⁰⁻² **TO HOLD s.o. accountable** (ə'kaʊntəbəl) jdn. zur Verantwortung ziehen — **unarmed** unbewaffnet — **to capture** ('kæptʃə) einfangen; h.: widerspiegeln — **expletive** (ɪk'spliːtɪv) Schimpfwort — **to get tired of s.th.** etw. leid sein — **footage** ('fʊtɪdʒ) Videoaufnahmen — **gratitude** ('grætɪtjuːd) Dankbarkeit — **through the grace of God** durch Gottes Gnade — **police brutality** polizeiliche Übergriffe

³⁻⁵ **to subdue** (səb'djuː) bändigen — **to detain** zurückhalten; festnehmen — **hoodie** Kapuzenpullover — **to choke** würgen — **to mistake s.o.** jdn. verwechseln — **laundering operation** ('lɔːndərɪŋ) h.: Geldwäsche — **Memorial Day** Volkstrauertag in den USA — **domestic incident** häuslicher Zwischenfall — **multiple** mehrere — **to tackle s.o.** h.: jdn. packen — **in broad daylight** am helllichten Tag

⁶⁻⁷ **exasperated** (ɪg'zɑːspəreɪtɪd) aufgebracht — **to honor s.o.** ('ɒnə) jdn. würdigen — **to pass** h.: sterben — **playoff win** Playoff-Sieg — **at length** ausführlich — **to speak out** s. äußern — **post-game press conference** Pressekonferenz nach dem Spiel — **to call for s.th.** etw. fordern — **to detail** (detailliert) beschreiben — **to distrust s.o.** jdm. misstrauen — **law enforcement** (ɪn'fɔːsmənt) Polizei

8 "You have no idea how that cop that day left the house," James said. "You don't know if he woke up on this side of the bed. You don't know if he woke up on the wrong side of the bed. You don't know if he had an argument at home with his significant other. You don't know if one of his kids said something to him, and he left the house steaming. Or maybe he just left the house saying that today is going to be the end for one of these Black people. That's what it feels like." No wonder James said, "I got nothing nice to say about those cops at all."

9 Moments later, James detailed what reforms need to happen so that police are held accountable when they kill unarmed Black people. First, James argued, the entry-level requirements need to change. "I don't want to sit here and say, 'I know what should be done.' But I did see one thing about the level of time in the academy before you become a police officer," James said. "We got kids going to college three and four years, six years to get their master's [degree], or they even go again, and they still didn't even get the opportunity at the workspace or the job that they actually want to get. But we have people going into the academy becoming police officers in a year or two."

10 Secondly, James called for gun reform. "Firearms are a huge issue in America," James said. "I

don't know how you clean that up. I'm not saying that I've got all the answers, but guns are a huge issue in America. They're not used for just hunting, which a lot of people do for sport. Right now, for Black people right now, when you're hunting, we think you're hunting us. Unfortunately, there's just too many killings going on. Not only from the cops, but we also have our own thing that we got to deal with, that we gotta get better at as well, with Black-on-Black crime."

11 Perhaps some of these changes can happen through the polls. That partly explains why James founded "More than a Vote," an organization aimed to improve voter registration and reduce voter suppression in the Black community. James added the organization has partnered with the NAACP to enroll young people to help as poll workers to protect the elderly from the coronavirus. Nonetheless, James stressed that change "doesn't only end in November, but it starts there" on Election Day.

12 "Being organized and having a plan and keeping our feet on the gas pedal is something that we've got to do," James said. "I know I'm all over the place, but my emotions are all over the place as well."

8–10 **to wake up on this side/the wrong side of the bed** mit dem richtigen/falschen Fuß aufstehen — **significant other** Lebensgefährte(-in) — **steaming** h.: wütend — **entry-level requirements** (ɪrˈkwaɪəmənts) Zugangsvoraussetzungen — **academy** h.: Polizeischule — **master's degree** Magisterabschluss — **workspace** Arbeitsplatz — **firearms** Schusswaffen — **to clean up** h.: in Ordnung bringen — **Black-on-Black crime** Verbrechen, bei denen sowohl Opfer als auch Täter Schwarze sind

11–12 **polls** (pəʊlz) Wahlen; s.w.u. **poll worker** Wahlhelfer(in) — **voter registration** Wählerregistrierung; s.w.u. **v. suppression** (səˈpreʃən) Unterdrückung von Wählern — **to partner with s.o.** s. mit jdm. zus.tun — **NAACP = National Association for the Advancement of Colored People** — **to enroll** h.: rekrutieren — **the elderly** Senioren — **nonetheless** (ˌ--ˈ-) nichtsdestotrotz — **to keep one's foot on the gas pedal** den Fuß nicht vom Gaspedal nehmen — **to be all over the place** h.: völlig durcheinander sein

---

How to Watch Police Shows in the Age of Black Lives Matter

TV SHOWS The crime genre glorifies police violence.
But should we ban such shows or reappraise them with a critical eye, asks Elias Rodriques.

1 IN A 2017 EPISODE of *Brooklyn Nine-Nine*, the acclaimed police comedy show, Sergeant Terry Jeffords is racially profiled while walking in his own neighbourhood. He later tells his captain, Raymond Holt, who is also black, that he wants to lodge a complaint. Captain Holt responds that he should not; doing so will make it difficult for him to advance in the NYPD, which comes with the prospect of making an even bigger change.

2 This is also the route, Holt explains, that he

took: he endured years of abuse as the only black, gay detective to become police captain so that he might make the NYPD less racist and anti-queer. In either case, the culprit is clear: racism in the NYPD. The solution is equally clear: change from within.

3 This is one of the more progressive of the crime genre's Black Lives Matter episodes, by which I mean those episodes that were clearly written in response to the movement, which started in 2013, against a racist state and state-sponsored violence. Consider, for instance, the 2015 episode of *CSI: Cyber* in which the protagonists respond to a video of the police shooting an unarmed black man, only to discover that the cops did not kill him, absolving them of all guilt. (Other shows with BLM episodes include *Law and Order, Chicago PD*, and more.) By contrast, *Brooklyn Nine-Nine* seems radical.

4 Yet even this episode of *Brooklyn Nine-Nine* disseminates the myth that there are good cops and bad cops and that if there are enough good cops, the police will no longer kill us. This belief that police reform will end racist violence dates at least as far back as the 1950s, as political scientist Naomi Murakawa documents in *The First Civil Right*. It also runs counter to the demands to defund the police in cities across the United States and divert resources to useful ends, such as social work and healthcare. Even the best copaganda can't bring itself to ask for less investment in the police, let alone to limit its power.

5 The crime genre's general support of police has led some thinkers and writers to condemn such shows. In Color of Change's report *Normalizing Injustice*, Rashad Robinson writes in the foreword: "The crime genre glorifies, justifies, and normalizes the systematic violence and injustice meted out by police, making heroes out of police and prosecutors who engage in abuse, particularly against people of color." Consequently, the report recommends that crime shows ought to address state and state-sponsored racism and to hire more diverse staff with a wider variety of experiences of the prison industrial complex among other things. The industry on the whole, the report continues, should develop new standards for the crime genre and hold show-runners accountable for producing racist shows. ...

6 While I have neither an attachment to the crime genre nor any qualms with cancelling all such shows, I do think there is another option: viewing these shows critically and educating others to do the same. Just as the journalist and scholar Joan Morgan argued that feminists can listen to hip-hop without accepting or reproducing its sexism, so, too, can audiences watch the crime genre while rejecting its racist premises.

7 Consider, for instance, James Baldwin's writing about the famous 1967 cop film, *In the Heat of the Night*. The film stars Sidney Poitier as a Philadelphia detective working on a case in Mississippi, who is subjected to racism from the locals and from

Snoop Dogg *and Mariska Hargitay seen on location for Law & Order: Special Victims Unit in New York City in 2019.* | PHOTO: *Getty Images*

his white partner while solving a crime. The racist partner eventually comes to respect Poitier; the force may be anti-black, the film admits, but one good black detective in pursuit of justice is enough to change the mind of one white racist and, perhaps, the world. After Baldwin notes all the ways in which the movie was wildly implausible, he writes, "a black man, in any case, had certainly best not believe everything he sees in the movies".

8 We need to teach more viewers to be like Baldwin because the troubling beliefs upholding the prison industrial complex are not just limited to the crime genre. Many 20th-century African-American novels, for instance, upheld and disseminated the ➜

0–2 **CRIME GENRE** ('ʒɑːrə) Krimi-Genre — **to glorify** ('glɔːrɪfaɪ) verherrlichen — **to reappraise** (ˌriːə'preɪz) neu bewerten — **acclaimed** (ə'kleɪmd) hochgelobt — **to be racially profiled** ('reɪʃəli) Opfer von Racial Profiling werden — **captain** h.: Vorgesetzte(r) — **to lodge a complaint** e-e Beschwerde einreichen — **to advance** h.: aufsteigen — **antiqueer** schwulenfeindlich — **in either case** in beiden Fällen — **culprit** ('kʌlprɪt) Schuldige(r); h.: Ursache — **equally** ('iːkwəli) genauso

3 **movement** Bewegung — **state-sponsored violence** ('vaɪələns) staatl. geförderte Gewalt — **protagonist** (prə'tægənɪst) Hauptfigur — **unarmed** unbewaffnet — **to absolve s.o. of s.th.** (əb'zɒlv) jdn. von etw. freisprechen

4 **to disseminate** (dɪ'semɪneɪt) verbreiten — **myth** Mythos; Irrglaube — **to document** dokumentieren — **civil right** Bürgerrecht — **to run counter to s.th.** etw. zuwiderlaufen — **to defund s.th.** etw. die Finanzierung entziehen — **to divert** (daɪ'vɜːt) umleiten — **end** h.: Zweck — **healthcare** Gesundheitsversorgung — **copaganda** Wortkreuzung aus „cop" und „propaganda" — **to bring o.s. to do s.th.** s. zu etw. durchringen — **let alone** geschweige denn

5 **to lead s.o. to do s.th.** jdn. zu etw. veranlassen — **thinker** Denker(in) — **to condemn s.th.** (kən'dem) etw. verurteilen — **injustice** (ɪn'dʒʌstɪs) Ungerechtigkeit — **foreword** Vorwort — **to mete out s.th.** (miːt) (fig) etw. austeilen — **prosecutor** ('prɒsɪkjuːtə) Staatsanwalt(-anwältin) — **to engage in s.th.** s. an etw. beteiligen — **people of color** Menschen, die nicht weiß sind — **to address s.th.** etw. thematisieren — **prison industrial complex** h.: Zus.hang zwischen der steigenden Anzahl Gefängnisinsassen und dem polit. Einfluss privater Gefängnisunternehmen, die staatl. Behörden Waren und Dienstleistungen bereitstellen — **to hold s.o. accountable** (ə'kaʊntəbəl) jdn. zur Verantwortung ziehen — **show-runner** Showrunner (Person, die das Tagesgeschäft e-r Fernsehserie verantwortet)

6–7 **attachment** h.: Vorliebe — **qualms** (kwɑːmz) Skrupel — **scholar** ('skɒlə) Wissenschaftler(in) — **to reproduce** reproduzieren — **premise** ('premɪs) Prämisse; Voraussetzung — *In the Heat of the Night* dt. Titel: *In der Hitze der Nacht* — **to be subjected to s.th.** etw. ausgesetzt sein — **locals** Einheimische — **force** h.: Polizei — **to be in pursuit of s.th.** (pə'sjuːt) nach etw. streben — **wildly implausible** (ɪm'plɔːzəbəl) völlig unglaubwürdig

8 **troubling** bedenklich — **to uphold** (-'-) aufrechterhalten —

myth that police violence only affects black men. In *The Long Dream* (1958), Richard Wright represents such violence as castration, while Ralph Ellison's *Invisible Man* (1951) gives no attention to the historical incident of police violence against Margie Polite in its representation of the Harlem riot of 1943, which Polite's treatment sparked. Critical reading and viewing, in other words, can succeed even where popular culture fails.

9 To better interrogate cultural material about the police, people need to be better educated about them as well as about what police and prison abolition means: uprooting the prison industrial complex and producing new systems to keep people safe and hold people accountable.

10 For those looking for a place to start, read black feminist scholars and activists such as Beth Richie, Mariame Kaba, and Andrea Ritchie, who have revealed the police's racist, sexist, and anti-queer distribution of violence. And read Angela Davis and Ruth Wilson Gilmore, whose work on abolition has made it possible to imagine a world without the prison industrial complex, a world other than the one that crime shows insist we must live in. After you've done so, regardless of whether or not you laugh at the episode of *Brooklyn Nine-Nine*, you'll know not to believe everything you see.

© *2020 Guardian News and Media Ltd*

The Long Dream dt. Titel: *Der schwarze Traum* — **to represent** h.: darstellen; s.w.u. **representation** Darstellung — *The Invisible Man* (ɪnˈvɪzəbəl) dt. Titel: *Der unsichtbare Mann* — **to give no attention** keine Beachtung schenken — **riot** (ˈraɪət) Aufstand — **to spark s.th.** (fig) etw. entfachen
9–10 **to interrogate** (ɪnˈterəgeɪt) h.: hinterfragen — **abolition** (ˌæbəˈlɪʃən) Abschaffung — **to uproot** (ʌpˈruːt) entwurzeln; h.: beseitigen — **place to start** h.: Einstieg — **distribution** (ˌdɪstrɪˈbjuːʃən) Verteilung — **other than** anders als — **regardless of s.th.** unabhängig von etw.

How the Music Industry Reckoned with Race This Year

MUSIC Black Lives Matter sparked overdue changes – but if deeper prejudices go unaddressed, they could be all too fleeting, says Chanté Joseph.

1 "IN THE WAKE of George Floyd" is a sentence I have both read and written too many times this year. His brutal and racist killing forced an elevated conscience across every industry: suddenly, organisations cared about Black lives and everyone wanted to amplify Black voices.

2 The global music industry acknowledged the tragic event in May particularly strongly because so many global superstars, if not Black themselves, are influenced by Black music. Universal Music Group duly pledged $25m towards a "change fund", while both Sony and Warner Music each pledged $100m for social justice and anti-racist causes – laudable but ultimately minuscule compared with the value Black artists and creatives have brought to the industry.

3 In light of this, Atlantic Records executives Brianna Agyemang and Jamila Thomas launched #TheShowMustBePaused. The initiative held a "Blackout Tuesday" that sought to allow the music

Tyler, the Creator, *accepts the International Male Solo Artist award during The BRIT Awards 2020.* | PHOTO: *Getty Images*

0–1 **TO RECKON with s.th.** h.: etw. aufarbeiten — **to spark s.th.** etw. entzünden; h.: etw. auslösen — **to go unaddressed** nicht thematisiert werden — **fleeting** flüchtig — **in the wake of s.th.** als Folge von etw. — **elevated conscience** (ˈkɒnʃəns) geschärftes Bewusstsein — **to amplify** (ˈæmplɪfaɪ) (ver)stärken
2 **to acknowledge s.th.** (əkˈnɒlɪdʒ) etw. würdigen — **duly** h.: umgehend — **to pledge** zusagen — **fund** Fonds — **cause** h.: Zweck — **laudable** (ˈlɔːdəbəl) lobenswert — **minuscule** (ˈmɪnəskjuːl) winzig
3 **in light of this** angesichts dessen — **executive** (ɪgˈzekjətɪv) Manager(in) — **to seek s.th.** etw. anstreben — **to reflect on s.th** über etw. nachdenken — **injustice** (ɪnˈdʒʌstɪs) Ungerechtigkeit — **multibillion-dollar** milliardenschwer — **predominantly** (prɪˈdɒmɪnəntli) überwiegend — **to hold s.o. accountable** (əˈkaʊntəbəl) jdn. zur Verantwortung ziehen — **at large** als Ganzes

industry to reflect on the injustices faced by Black people. "The music industry is a multibillion-dollar industry. An industry that has profited predominantly from Black art," their website reads. "Our mission is to hold accountable the industry at large, including major corporations and their partners, who benefit from the efforts, struggles, and successes of Black people."

4 The day of action also spread beyond the music industry, as social media users all over the globe performatively posted black squares in solidarity with Black people. It almost felt comical: influencers who had been silent on Black struggle now offering a silent protest.

5 White people loudly "doing the work" they should already have been doing wasn't the only thing that changed. Black artists, given a licence to create politically charged music with less fear of a backlash or blacklisting, created sounds and visuals that reflected the times. Terrace Martin, Denzel Curry, Kamasi Washington, G Perico, and Daylyt teamed up on "Pig Feet", a track that incorporated live recordings from the protests and embodied their energy. …

6 Black Lives Matter also gave Black artists the space to talk about the racism that they had faced. X Factor winner Alexandra Burke was told she needed to bleach her skin; Misha B said she was left feeling suicidal after being accused of bullying on the same show; Sugababes' Keisha Buchanan needed therapy after the "trauma" she experienced in the industry. The year threw up stories like this that we all knew deep down to be true but had never been told in public.

7 Another watershed was reached regarding the word "urban" to describe Black music. It has been a contested label since the 80s, used to sell Black music to white audiences and radio stations, pigeonholing black artists with little regard for the music they make. "Whenever we – and I mean guys that look like me – do anything that's genre-bending, they always put it in the rap or urban category," Tyler, the Creator said at the Grammys in January. (This goes both ways: when Lil Nas X's "Old Town Road" was released in 2019, it wasn't allowed in the overwhelmingly white country charts.)

8 On 5 June, Republic Records, home to artists such as Taylor Swift, Ariana Grande, and the Weeknd, announced it would no longer be using the term urban, saying: "It is important to shape the future of what we want it to look like and not

Brianna Agyemang *and Jamila Thomas accept the Executives of the Year Award during Billboard Women in Music 2020.* | PHOTO: *Getty Images*

adhere to the outdated structures of the past." Shortly after, the Grammys announced they would stop using "urban" in its award categories.

9 These successes, though, are still outweighed by much larger injustices faced by Black musicians. In a viral Instagram post on Blackout Tuesday, academic and writer Josh Kun wrote: "If the music industry wants to support Black lives, labels and platforms can start with amending contracts, distributing royalties, diversifying boardrooms, and retroactively paying back all the Black artists and their families they have built their empires on." His post touched on an issue that is racialised: young Black artists from low socioeconomic backgrounds often take deeply unfair record deals.

10 There is a lack of sympathy for Black artists, too: there was endless support for Taylor Swift when she was attempting to buy back her masters from Scooter Braun, but when Megan Thee Stallion spoke about her label 1501's unwillingness to renegotiate her deal, many on social media turned into scornful experts on contract law.

11 Moreover, when she was allegedly shot by Tory Lanez (who has since been charged over the incident), the internet was rife with unforgiving and judgmental opinions on Megan. "Black women are so unprotected & we hold so many things in to protect the feelings of others [without] considering our own," she wrote on Twitter. People questioned why she didn't report the incident to the police when they arrived on the scene, but she explained ⮕

⁴⁻⁶ **performatively** (pəˈfɔːmətɪvli) performativ — **politically charged** politisch brisant — **backlash** Gegenreaktion — **to blacklist s.o.** jdn. auf die schwarze Liste setzen — **visuals** (ˈvɪʒuəlz) Bilder — **to incorporate** (ɪnˈkɔːpəreɪt) einbeziehen — **to embody** (fig) verkörpern — **to bleach** bleichen; h.: aufhellen — **suicidal** (ˌsuːɪˈsaɪdəl) suizidgefährdet — **bullying** (ˈbʊlɪŋ) Mobbing — **to throw up** h.: hervorbringen

⁷⁻⁸ **watershed** (fig) Wendepunkt — **contested** umstritten — **to pigeonhole s.o.** (ˈpɪdʒənhəʊl) jdn. in e-e bestimmte Schublade stecken — **with little regard for** ohne Rücksicht auf — **genre-bending** (ˈʒɑ̃ːrə,--) genreübergreifend — **to shape** (fig) gestalten — **to adhere to s.th.** (ədˈhɪə) an etw. festhalten

⁹ **to outweigh** (ˌ-ˈweɪ) überwiegen — **to amend** (əˈmend) nachbessern — **royalties** (ˈrɔɪəltiz) Tantiemen — **to diversify** (daɪˈvɜːsɪfaɪ) diversifizieren; s.w.u. **ethnic diversity** ethnische Vielfalt — **boardroom** Vorstandsetage — **retroactively** (ˌretrəʊˈæktɪvli) rückwirkend — **to touch on an issue** ein Problem ansprechen — **racialised** (ˈreɪʃəlaɪzd) durch die Hautfarbe bestimmt — **socioeconomic** (ˌsəʊsiəʊˌekəˈnɒmɪk) sozioökonomisch

¹⁰ **to buy back** zurückkaufen — **masters** h.: Master-Aufnahmen — **unwillingness** (ʌnˈwɪlɪŋnəs) fehlende Bereitschaft — **to renegotiate** (ˌriːnəˈgəʊʃieɪt) neu verhandeln — **scornful** (ˈskɔːnfəl) höhnisch — **contract law** Vertragsrecht

¹¹ **allegedly** (əˈledʒɪdli) mutmaßlich — **to charge s.o.** jdn. anklagen — **rife with** voll von — **unforgiving** gnadenlos — **judgmental** (dʒʌdʒˈmentəl) abschätzig — **to hold s.th. in** h.: etw. unterdrücken — **to consider s.th.** (kənˈsɪdə) h.: auf

⮕ on Instagram Live that this was to protect both of them, given the "aggressiveness" of the LAPD and the history of police brutality even towards victims. …

12 Black artists still go shortchanged, mislabelled, and unrecognised in other genres, such as dance music. There has been a historic lack of accreditation for Black women dance vocalists despite them helping to shape the sound, and misogynoir still plagues dance music.

13 In *Mixmag's* Blackout series, five Black women detailed their experiences within the music industry, particularly in dance, and described worrying patterns of not only racism but colourism, fatphobia, and erasure. In the same series of articles, the house music pioneer Marshall Jefferson wrote about how he quit DJing because of the difficulties Black DJs faced in the industry, particularly regarding recognition and fair pay.

14 It has been an eye-opening year for the industry. Uncomfortable conversations about severe imbalances of power and the exploitation of Black artists are finally taking place. UK Music's 2020 diversity report showed a rise in ethnic diversity in the industry over the last two years (though the rise was much slower at senior levels), and the formation of groups such as Black Music Coalition will help to maintain that drive for change.

15 But as "the wake of George Floyd" calms, Black artists could so easily be silenced once more, entertaining the white masses while feeling unable to complain about racism for fear of being seen as ungrateful. Any structural changes made this year in response to racism and police brutality, meanwhile, sit within wider capitalist structures.

16 As long as Black communities suffer from systemic poverty and neglect, artists from these communities – without adequate legal support or relevant connections – will be easily exploited. And as long as racism exists in society – as long as society is set up in a racist way – it will underpin and inform the music industry.

17 Music executives and labels have demonstrated compassion and care this year, but they must continue to act – and go further than the rest of society. By elevating the Black artists and staff that are innate to its success, the industry is well placed to make itself an example to others. But it is not enough to give Black people a voice if they can't speak their truth.

© 2020 Guardian News and Media Ltd

---

etw. Rücksicht nehmen — **aggressiveness** Aggressivität

¹²⁻¹³ **shortchanged** (ˌ-ˈ-) ausgenutzt — **mislabelled** (ˌmɪsˈleɪbəld) abgestempelt — **unrecognized** (ˌʌnˈrekəgnaɪzd) verkannt — **accreditation** (əˌkredɪˈteɪʃən); s.w.u. **recognition** (ˌrekəgˈnɪʃən) h.: Anerkennung — **vocalist** Sänger(in) — **misogynoir** (mɪˈsɒdʒənwɑː) Feindlichkeit gegenüber schwarzen Frauen — **to plague** (pleɪg) (fig) plagen — **colourism** (ˈkʌlərɪzəm) Diskriminierung aufgrund der Hautfarbe — **fatphobia** Fettphobie — **erasure** (ɪˈreɪʒə) Unsichtbarkeit (als subtile Form der Diskriminierung)

¹⁴⁻¹⁵ **imbalance of power** Machtgefälle — **exploitation** Ausbeutung — **at senior levels** in den Chefetagen — **formation** h.: Gründung — **to silence s.o.** jdn. mundtot machen — **ungrateful** undankbar — **to sit within s.th.** h.: in etw. eingebettet sein

¹⁶⁻¹⁷ **neglect** (nɪˈglekt) Vernachlässigung — **to underpin** (ˌ--ˈ-) h.: beeinflussen — **to inform** h.: durchdringen — **compassion** Mitgefühl — **to elevate s.o.** (ˈelɪveɪt) h.: jdn. fördern — **innate** (ɪˈneɪt) angeboren; h.: wesentlich

---

Lewis Hamilton Says BLM Protest Is Human Rights Issue, not about Politics

RACING The F1 racing driver expects new rules to ban a repeat of his T-shirt protest, writes Giles Richards.

1 LEWIS HAMILTON has insisted his support for anti-racism and protests against incidences of racial injustice will not be inhibited by any new FIA rulings. Hamilton attracted controversy at the last meeting at Mugello by wearing a T-shirt bearing the words "Arrest the cops that killed Breonna Taylor" before and after the race.

2 Speaking in the buildup to this weekend's Russian Grand Prix, where the FIA is expected to clarify rules on what drivers can and cannot wear, Hamilton restated his determination to continue pursuing what he described as a human rights issue rather than a political point. "I don't know what they [the FIA] are going to do this weekend," he said. "Lots of rules have been written for me over the years, and they haven't stopped me."

3 Since the Tuscan Grand Prix, there has been expectation that the FIA would react to Hamilton's protest against the death of Taylor, the 26-year-old who was shot dead in her home by police in Kentucky.

4 Hamilton has been a strident supporter of the Black Lives Matter movement and wore the T-shirt as a pre-race, anti-racism gesture in Mugello and again for the podium ceremony after his victory. The FIA is a signatory to the Olympic charter which forbids any form of demonstration or political, religious, or racial propaganda.

Lewis Hamilton *at Mugello Circuit in Italy in September 2020.* | PHOTO: *Getty Images*

5   In Sochi, Hamilton was unapologetic. "I don't regret a single moment of it," he said. "I follow my heart and do what is right, and that was me following my heart. I did something that has never really happened in F1, and obviously they will stop it from happening moving forwards.

6   "People talk about sport not being a place for politics, but ultimately it is a human rights issue, and that is something we should be pushing towards. We have a huge, amazing group of people that watch our sport from different backgrounds and cultures, and we should be pushing positive messages towards them, especially for equality."

7   He said he had not spoken with the FIA. Hamilton has led the call for change since the killing of George Floyd, and his stance has encouraged other drivers to speak out and for F1 to adopt a strong, public anti-racism stance. The world champion conceded that the process was one that was evolving across F1 but also stressed he believed his actions in wearing the T-shirt had proved to be a potent weapon in drawing attention to racial injustice.

8   "This is a learning process for everyone," he said. "People have been happy with the norm here of how life and society has operated, but the world and the younger generation in particular are more conscious that things aren't equal and that change is needed. It takes conversations with people and things like Mugello to spark a conversation that perhaps would never have taken place."

9   He was also unsure that the FIA has yet fully grasped the importance of the cause he is championing nor how difficult it might be. "I will continue to work with them, but do I believe they fully understand? I don't know. Perhaps in the future, we all will to the same extent," he added. "It's not something that is going to change overnight. It will take a long, long time. It won't be over in my career or even in my lifetime, but the goal is to change things for future generations."

⁰⁻¹ **F1 RACING DRIVER** Formel-1-Rennfahrer(in) — **repeat** Wiederholung — **incidence** ('ınsıdəns) Vorfall — **injustice** (ın'dʒʌstıs) Ungerechtigkeit — **to inhibit s.o.** (ın'hıbıt) jdn. (be)hindern — **FIA = Fédération Internationale de l'Automobile** Dachverband der Automobilclubs und Motorsport-Vereine — **rulings** Entscheidungen — **meeting** h.: Rennen — **bearing the words** mit der Aufschrift

²⁻³ **in the buildup** h.: im Vorfeld — **Russian Grand Prix** Großer Preis von Russland — **to clarify** ('klærıfaı) klären — **to restate** (-'-) bekräftigen — **to pursue s.th.** (pə'sjuː); s.w.u. **to champion s.th.** h.: s. für etw. einsetzen — **Tuscan Grand Prix** ('tʌskən) Großer Preis der Toskana — **to shoot s.o. dead** jdn. erschießen

⁴⁻⁵ **strident** ('straıdənt) vehement — **movement** Bewegung — **pre-race** vor dem Rennen — **gesture** ('dʒestʃə) Geste — **podium ceremony** Siegerehrung — **signatory** ('sıgnətəri) Unterzeichner(in) — **Olympic charter** Olympische Charta — **to be unapologetic** (ˌʌnəpɒlə'dʒetık) s. nicht entschuldigen (wollen) — **to follow one's heart** auf sein Herz hören — **moving forwards** h.: in Zukunft

⁶⁻⁷ **ultimately** ('ʌltımətli) letztlich — **to push towards s.th.** h.: auf etw. hinwirken; s.w.u. **to push** h.: vermitteln — **equality** (i'kwɒləti) Gleichberechtigung — **call for change** Ruf nach Veränderung — **stance** Haltung; Meinung — **to speak out** s. zu Wort melden — **to concede** (kən'siːd) eingestehen — **to evolve** (ı'vɒlv) s. entwickeln — **potent** wirkungsvoll — **weapon** h.: Mittel

⁸⁻⁹ **to spark a conversation** e-e Diskussion anstoßen — **to grasp s.th.** etw. begreifen — **cause** Anliegen — **to the same extent** im gleichen Maße — **overnight** von heute auf morgen

27

White Celebs Rush to Amplify Black Lives Matter. The Results Are Mixed to Embarrassing.

CELEBRITIES As a white person, you cannot expect applause whenever you speak out against a system from which you have benefited, says Mary McNamara.

1 WHITE CELEBRITIES, influencers, commentators, and just regular folks are having a prolonged and very public deer-in-the-headlights moment. As protests against racism and police brutality continue to grow in every state and around the world, white people with media platforms (including me) find themselves caught between the Scylla of silence and the Charybdis of potential cringe call-out.

2 As the video of George Floyd's death under the knee of Minneapolis Police Officer Derek Chauvin sent hundreds of thousands into the street to protest, many celebrities, some of them white, spoke out. Amid the early coverage of these protests, which focused primarily on violence and property damage rather than peaceful demonstrators, many of these advocates then found themselves being denounced for supporting violence.

Denouncing police brutality and supporting Black Lives Matter

3 As the media shifted focus and made it clear that the protests were vastly peaceful, more stars in entertainment and social media began denouncing police brutality and supporting Black Lives Matter. Those who couched their support in a call for an end to violence, which implied that the protesters were to blame for that violence, were often called out; those who said nothing were criticized for their silence.

4 Earlier this month, #BlackoutTuesday turned into a big fail when social media influencers and stars redefined "the least I can do" by filling their social media platforms with black boxes. The initiative, designed to target the music industry, was created by two black music marketers who asked that music platforms like Spotify, Apple, and Tik-Tok cease operations for a day to show support for the community that in many ways created them. When a much larger array of people participated, adding #BlackLivesMatter and #BLM to their posts, the barrage of black boxes ended up drowning out activists and organizers, many still engaged actively in protesting.

Late night shows are a bastion of whiteness

5 Social media influencers, many of them young and inexperienced at addressing issues outside their personal lives or whatever niche they had established, were encouraged to use their platforms to support the protests and Black Lives Matter, and those who did not were told that if they didn't have anything constructive to say, they should stop saying anything at all.

6 Late-night hosts, who often act as cultural first responders during times of crisis, were among the first caught in those headlights. But there is no getting around the fact that, with the exception of Trevor Noah, late night is, and always has been, a bastion of whiteness. Which is why Noah's own early response to the protests – "Think about that unease that you felt watching that Target being looted. Try to imagine how it must feel for black Americans when they watch themselves being looted every single day" – and his recent insistence ➨

0–1 **CELEBS** (sə'lebs) Promis — **to amplify** ('æmplɪfaɪ) verstärken; h.: unterstützen; s.w.u. **amplification** — **to speak out against s.th.** s. gegen etw. aussprechen — **prolonged** anhaltend — **deer-in-the-headlights moment** (fig) Schreckstarre; s.w.u. **to be caught in the headlights** (fig) in Schreckstarre verfallen — **to be caught between Scylla and Charybdis** ('sɪlə; kə'rɪbdɪs) in der Zwickmühle stecken — **cringe call-out** (krɪndʒ) Anprangerung wg. peinlichen Verhaltens

2–3 **amid** (ə'mɪd) vor dem Hintergrund — **coverage** ('kʌvərɪdʒ) Berichterstattung — **advocate** ('ædvəkət) Fürsprecher(in) — **to denounce** (dɪ'naʊns) beschuldigen; anprangern — **vastly** weitgehend — **to couch** (kaʊtʃ) (fig) kleiden; hüllen — **call for s.th.** Ruf nach etw. — **to imply** (ɪm'plaɪ) implizieren; s.w.u. **implicit** (ɪm'plɪsɪt) impliziert — **to be to blame for s.th.** an etw. schuld sein — **to call s.o. out** jdn. anprangern

4 **fail** Reinfall — **to redefine** (‚--'-) neu definieren — **to target s.th.**; s.w.u. **to aim at s.th.** auf etw. abzielen — **marketer** Marketingspezialist(in) — **to cease operations** (si:s) den Betrieb einstellen — **array** (ə'reɪ) h.: Anzahl — **barrage** ('bærɑːʒ) (fig) Flut — **to drown s.o. out** jdn. übertönen — **to be engaged in s.th.** mit etw. beschäftigt sein

5–6 **to address s.th.** etw. thematisieren — **niche** (niːʃ) Nische — **late-night host** Moderator(in) e-r Late-Night-Show — **first responder** Ersthelfer(in) — **times of crisis** Krisenzeiten — **there is no getting around s.th.** etw. lässt sich nicht leugnen — **bastion** (fig) Bastion — **unease** (ʌn'iːz) Unbehagen — **to loot** plündern — **insistence** (ɪn'sɪstəns) Forderung

7–8 **high-profile** prominent — **to turn s.th. over** h.: etw. übergeben — **PSA = Public Service Announcement**

⊃ that Joe Biden define "police reform" have been so powerful.

7 More recently, a group of high-profile white women, including Sen. Elizabeth Warren, Hillary Clinton, Julia Roberts, and Gwyneth Paltrow, turned over their Instagram accounts for #SharetheMicNow, while another group of white celebrities participated in a video PSA in which they each vow to "Take Responsibility" for their complicity in our country's systemic racism.

8 The results were mixed to embarrassing. The concept of "sharing the mic" is fine as far as it goes, and one hopes that followers of the white famous women will become followers of the black not-as-famous women. But that kind of amplification only works if it is sustained – that is, black women get big mics of their own. As for the "Take Responsibility" video, well, even in these Zoom-conditioned times, it is virtually impossible to watch without cringing.

Listen to criticism and do better next time

9 But criticizing the participants, or their choice of eyewear, is not helpful either. When folks like Aaron Paul and Bryce Dallas Howard were asked if they wanted to join with the NAACP for this PSA – aimed at making white people who proudly identify as nonracist recognize their implicit role in a racist society – were they supposed to say no? How can you refuse to be in a PSA against racism?

10 You can't. As many have suggested since the PSA's airing, you could take care not to impose a "white savior" ethos on your remarks, but you can't ask for final director's cut. So you just do the best you can and sit quietly while everyone slays you for it. You listen to the criticism, don't take it personally, and then do better next time.

11 Because there has to be a next time. Or a first time. As a white person, you cannot expect emoji hearts and applause whenever you speak out against a system from which you have benefited, unintentionally or not. Yes, you may have to screw up your courage to do it, but that doesn't make it an inherently courageous act. Speak out because it is right and because the survival of this country and your immortal soul depend on it.

12 Fear of being called out or "misunderstood" or being seen as "political" isn't a legitimate excuse. Staying silent because you're afraid you'll put your foot in your mouth is even worse. If you don't know how to discuss racism at this point, it's time to learn, even if it means learning through your mistakes. Yes, you may be judged on Twitter, but freedom from being judged on Twitter is not a constitutionally guaranteed right; freedom from being brutalized by law enforcement and/or unlawfully detained is. …

Speak out thoughtfully and without fear of failure

13 During the #MeToo movement, many men felt very uncomfortable, caught between a legitimate desire to support women and the defensive need to point out that not all men are predators – wanting terrible people to be punished but also worried that #MeToo was going too far, denouncing too wide a swath of behavior.

14 But complaints about being uncomfortable and arguing that it was "a few bad apples" didn't stand then and doesn't stand now; most police officers may not actively engage in racist abuse, just as most movie executives may not actively prey on the women around them. But the culture is designed to protect the bad apples – to, in some cases, reward the bad apples. So, if you're not willing to dismantle that culture, then you are part of the problem. …

15 If you are a person with a public platform, or even if you are not, you need to speak out. Thoughtfully and without fear of failure, because the only real failure at this point is silence.

Werbespot, der das Bewusstsein der Öffentlichkeit für ein bestimmtes Thema schärfen soll — **to vow** (vaʊ) geloben — **complicity** (kəmˈplɪsəti) Mitschuld — **systemic racism** institutioneller Rassismus — **mic** (maɪk) Mikrofon — **as far as it goes** so weit — **to sustain** aufrechterhalten — **Zoom-conditioned** durch Zoom geprägt — **to cringe** s. fremdschämen

9–10 **participant** (pɑːˈtɪsɪpənt) Mitwirkende(r) — **eyewear** (ˈaɪweə) Brille — **NAACP = National Association for the Advancement of Colored People** — **airing** Ausstrahlung — **to impose** h.: (fig) überstülpen — **"white savior" ethos** (ˈiːθɒs) Weißer-Retter-Ethos — **to slay s.o.** (fig) jdn. niedermachen

11–12 **unintentionally** (ˌʌnɪnˈtenʃənəli) ungewollt — **to screw up one's courage** all seinen Mut zus.nehmen — **inherently** (ɪnˈherəntli) an sich — **immortal** unsterblich — **to put one's foot in one's mouth** ins Fettnäpfchen treten — **to judge s.o.** über jdn. urteilen — **constitutionally** (ˌkɒnstɪˈtjuːʃənəli) verfassungsmäßig — **to brutalize s.o.** (ˈbruːtəlaɪz) jdn. brutal behandeln — **law enforcement** (ɪnˈfɔːsmənt) Polizei — **unlawfully** (ʌnˈlɔːfəli) unrechtmäßig — **to detain s.o.** jdn. festhalten

13–15 **movement** Bewegung — **uncomfortable** unbehaglich — **defensive** abwehrend — **predator** (ˈpredətə) Raubtier; h.: Sexualstraftäter(in) — **swath** (swɔθ) Schneise; h.: (fig) Spektrum — **a few bad apples** ein paar schwarze Schafe — **to stand** h.: standhalten — **movie executive** (ɪgˈzekjətɪv) Filmproduzent(in) — **to prey on s.o.** h.: jdn. belästigen — **to dismantle** demontieren — **thoughtfully** besonnen

Martin Luther King, Jr., *during the March on Washington in 1963.* | PHOTO: *Getty Images*

'He Was Extremely Radical'

CIVIL RIGHTS MOVEMENT

Martin Luther King's children talk to Oliver Laughland about their father's life and George Floyd's death.

1   WHEN FOOTAGE of George Floyd's death in Minneapolis, under the knee of a white police officer, was beamed around the world, Bernice King wept. She was five years old in 1968 when her father, Martin Luther King Jr, was killed by an assassin's bullet on a hotel balcony in Memphis. She was a year younger than Floyd's daughter Gianna. "You feel the pain of the loss," she says over a video call, a framed photograph of her father on the mantelpiece behind her. "Because you know what it did to you, too. And you can only imagine what it's doing to that little girl."

2   It is easy to trace the lines from the US's latest reckoning on race and police violence to the civil rights struggles of the 60s. Floyd's death started the largest wave of protest in the US since King's murder. But for some, the connections are as much lived reality as a point of historic reference.

3   Bernice's elder brother, Martin Luther King III,

was 10 at the time his father was killed. In June this year, he bowed his head in front of Floyd's golden casket during a memorial service. He also reflects on the children left behind. "When you are grieving, you appreciate all the love that the world provides for you," he says from his living room in Atlanta, in front of a large image of his mother, Coretta Scott King. "But, at some point, most people go back to their homes, and you're all alone, grieving by yourself. And you have to figure out how to navigate through the terrible pain."

4   In the aftermath of Floyd's death, as buildings burned in cities across the country, familiar arguments invoking King's legacy of nonviolence and civil disobedience were used to question the validity of mostly peaceful protests. Republican senators quoted King's words out of context, and memes circulated with images juxtaposing peaceful marches in the 60s and looting in 2020.

0–1   **CIVIL RIGHTS MOVEMENT** Bürgerrechtsbewegung — **footage** ('fʊtɪdʒ) Videoaufnahmen — **to beam** (aus) strahlen — **to weep** weinen — **assassin** (ə'sæsɪn) Attentäter(in); s.w.u. **assassination** Ermordung — **framed** gerahmt — **mantlepiece** Kaminsims

2–3   **to trace lines** (fig) Verbindungslinien ziehen — **reckoning on** (fig) Auseinandersetzung mit — **as much … as** sowohl … als auch — **point of reference** Bezugspunkt — **to bow one's head** (baʊ) s. verneigen — **casket** Sarg — **memorial service** Gedenkgottesdienst — **to reflect on s.th.** über etw. reflektieren — **to grieve** (griːv) trauern — **at some point** irgendwann — **to navigate** (fig) e-n Weg finden

4   **in the aftermath** infolge — **to invoke s.th.** s. auf etw. berufen — **legacy** ('legəsi) Vermächtnis — **nonviolence** (ˌ-'vaɪələns) Gewaltlosigkeit; s.w.u. **nonviolent** gewaltlos — **civil disobedience** (ˌdɪsə'biːdiəns) ziviler Ungehorsam; s.w.u. **to disobey s.th.** (ˌdɪsə'beɪ) etw. missachten — **validity** (və'lɪdəti) h.: Berechtigung — **quoted out of context** aus dem Zus.hang gerissen (**to quote** zitieren) — **to circulate** ('sɜːkjəleɪt) kursieren — **to juxtapose** (ˌdʒʌkstə'pəʊz) gegenüberstellen — **looting** Plünderung

5 King's children are used to this rewriting of history. Since his death, he has been repositioned in the mainstream American imagination as a unifying figure who defeated the segregationist south with peaceful nonviolence, driven by dreams of a future where his four children would "live in a nation where they will not be judged by the colour of their skin but by the content of their character".

6 There is truth in that depiction, but it also nullifies King's radicalism: his demands after the Civil Rights and Voting Rights acts were passed in 1964 and 1965 for universal income and a higher minimum wage; the brutality he and thousands of others endured as they put their bodies on the line; the surveillance he was placed under by J Edgar Hoover's FBI; and ultimately his assassination, which the King family believe was connected to a higher conspiracy. King was not popular among the broader American public at the time of his death.

7 "I think most people focus on 'I have a dream', and they don't even focus on the entire speech," says Martin. "You know, what got him killed was not talking about riding in the front of buses. He talked about a living wage … he talked about a radical redistribution of wealth, which definitely was frightening to those pursuing money.

8 "But the message has been sanitised by mainstream media because if you keep him in that sanitised version then you never realise the part of him that talked about a revolution of values. The irony of it is here we are today, and we still need a revolution of values."

9 Bernice says: "Anyone who talks about being a transformed nonconformist; anyone who talks about it being your duty to disobey unjust laws; anybody who talks about a nation that continues to spend millions and millions more on military defence over programmes of social uplift [as one is] approaching spiritual death: that's extremely radical to me." …

10 But how do they believe their father would have interpreted this moment, with its complicated entanglement of nonviolent protest, direct confrontation, and a militarised police response? "You know, Dad would never have condoned violence ever," says Martin. "But he didn't condemn it, either. Saying 'a riot is a language of the unheard' is saying: 'I understand why people are forced or pushed to riot.' People are so frustrated. People

Coretta Scott King, *wife of Martin Luther King, Jr., with their children Yolanda (8), Martin Luther King III (6), Dexter (3), and Bernice (11 months) in 1964.* | PHOTO: *Getty Images*

are so dehumanised and have been so abused that they have resorted to this."

11 The point was driven home to Martin when, shortly after Floyd's death, his 11-year-old daughter, Yolanda, informed her parents that she was too scared to go outside alone and play in case a police officer entered the back yard. "That broke my heart – that our daughter would be afraid of those that are supposed to protect and serve," he says. "We now have to sit down with her and figure out how she can differentiate between some policemen who are not good and the many who are good."

12 Although none of King's children knew their father as adults, his life's work inspired Martin and Bernice to continue the struggle. Bernice is a pastor and in 2009 was elected president of the Southern Christian Leadership Conference (SCLC) founded ➲

---

5   **to reposition** neu positionieren — **in the mainstream imagination** in der Volksmeinung — **unifying** einigend — **segregationist** (ˌsegrɪˈɡeɪʃənɪst) von Rassentrennung geprägt — **driven** (fig) angetrieben — **to judge s.o.** jdn. beurteilen

6   **depiction** Darstellung — **to nullify** (ˈnʌlɪfaɪ) annullieren; h.: ignorieren — **Civil Rights and Voting Rights acts** Bürgerrechts- und Wahlrechtsgesetz — **universal income** Grundeinkommen — **to put one's body on the line** sein Leben riskieren — **to place s.o. under surveillance** (səˈveɪləns) jdn. überwachen — **ultimately** (ˈʌltɪmətli) schließlich — **to be connected to s.th.** mit etw. in Verbindung stehen — **conspiracy** (kənˈspɪrəsi) Verschwörung

7–9   **living wage** existenzsichernder Lohn — **redistribution** (ˌriːdɪstrɪˈbjuːʃən) Umverteilung — **to pursue s.th.** (pəˈsjuː) nach etw. streben — **to sanitise** (ˈsænɪtaɪz) reinigen; h.: (fig) entschärfen — **irony** (ˈaɪrəni) Ironie — **nonconformist** (ˌ-kənˈfɔːmɪst) Nonkonformist(in) — **unjust** (ʌnˈdʒʌst) ungerecht — **over** h.: gegenüber; verglichen mit — **social uplift** sozialer Aufstieg

10   **entanglement** (ɪnˈtæŋɡəlmənt) Verstrickung — **to condone s.th.** etw. gutheißen — **to condemn s.th.** etw. verurteilen — **riot** (ˈraɪət) Aufruhr — **the unheard** die Ungehörten — **to push s.o. to do s.th.** jdn. zu etw. treiben — **dehumanised** (ˌdiːˈhjuːmənaɪzd) entmenschlicht — **abused** (əˈbjuːzd) misshandelt — **to resort to s.th.** auf etw. zurückgreifen

11–12   **to drive the point home** unmissverständlich klarmachen — **yard** h.: Garten; Hof — **to differentiate** (ˌdɪfəˈrenʃieɪt) unterscheiden — **Southern Christian Leadership Conference** Christliche Führungskonferenz des Sü-

"He was extremely radical"

by her father (although she did not take up the position). … She has delivered sermons and eulogies at many major civil rights commemorations, and she appears as a pundit on cable news.

13 Martin, who served as SCLC president for seven years, will on Friday lead a recreation of his father's 1963 March on Washington, alongside the Rev Al Sharpton. Among many other public appearances, he delivered an emotive speech at the 2008 Democratic convention, when Barack Obama became the party's first African-American presidential nominee.

14 As the oldest surviving sibling (Yolanda, King's first-born, died in 2007), Martin has the most lucid memories of his father. "He didn't have a large quantity of time," Martin says. "But the quality of time was remarkable." But, even as children, they were aware of the dangers their father faced. Martin recalls picking up the house telephone to hear "an ugly voice making threatening remarks". …

15 He remembers the night his father died in 1968. Bernice was asleep, but the other children were comforted by their mother. "She said: 'Your father is going home to live with God. When you see him, it will be as if he is asleep, but you won't be able to wake him up. He won't be able to hug and kiss you as you so often experienced.'"

16 Bernice, who learned of her father's significance to the world from her mother's teachings, experienced the trauma a little later, in early adulthood. "You have issues of abandonment and distrust," she says. "I think for me that has expressed itself in different phases of my life, where I've had a lot of walls up."

17 Although their father was killed more than half a century ago, Martin and Bernice still mourn him. The 50th anniversary proved particularly difficult to navigate. "I don't even know what triggers it, but there are still times that I grieve," says Martin. For Bernice, it can also be triggered by acts of racism and violence. "Just looking at the state of our world and kind of wishing that he and my mom were here, I have those moments over and over again where I just tear up and cry," she says. "It never leaves you."

---

dens — **to take up a position** ein Amt antreten — **sermon** Predigt — **eulogy** ('ju:lədʒi) Lobrede — **commemoration** Gedenkfeier — **pundit** ('pʌndɪt) Experte(-in)
13–14 **recreation** (fig) Neuauflage — **alongside s.o.** an der Seite von jdm. — **emotive** emotional — **Democratic convention** Parteitag der Demokraten — **presidential nominee** Präsidentschaftskandidat(in) — **siblings** Geschwister — **first-born** Erstgeborene(r) — **lucid** ('lu:sɪd) klar; deutlich — **threatening** ('θretənɪŋ) drohend
15–17 **to comfort s.o.** jdn. trösten — **significance** (sɪg'nɪfɪkəns) Bedeutung — **adulthood** ('ædʌlthʊd) Erwachsenenalter — **abandonment** (ə'bændənmənt) Verlassenwerden — **distrust** Misstrauen — **to have a lot of walls up** s. abschotten — **to mourn s.o.** (mɔːn) um jdn. trauern — **to trigger s.th.** etw. auslösen — **to tear up** Tränen in die Augen bekommen

Uncle Ben's Rice to Get Revamp after Criticism over Racial Stereotyping

BRANDING

Mars will drop the image of a black farmer from the brand, recognising it is 'out of step with the times', writes Rebecca Smithers.

1   UNCLE BEN'S is to change its name and branding, following criticism that its 70-year-old logo and imagery of a black farmer involved racial stereotyping.

2   The US rice brand will now be known as Ben's Original, with revamped packaging bearing the new name appearing in shops next year. The company's owner, Mars, said it understood the "inequities" associated with the product.

3   "Over several weeks, we have listened to thousands of consumers, our own associates, and other stakeholders from around the world," said Fiona

Dawson, a Mars executive. "We understand the inequities that were associated with the name and face of the previous brand, and as we announced in June, we have committed to change." Those conversations had led the company to settle on Ben's Original as the new name, she said, although the company is still deciding on an image to accompany the revamp.

4   Mars becomes one of several global food companies to agree to drop controversial racial imagery from its branding – a ripple effect from the Black Lives Matters protests sparked by the police killing of George Floyd in May.

5   In June, the Quaker food company announced plans to change the 130-year-old Aunt Jemima pancake and syrup name and logo. The character is an African-American woman who was originally dressed as a minstrel show performer.

6   Mars said in the summer that Uncle Ben was a fictional character whose name was first used in 1946 as a reference to an African-American Texan rice farmer. The image used on Uncle Ben packaging was a "beloved Chicago chef and waiter named Frank Brown", the company said. But it also recognised that the use of the character was out of step with the times and pledged to overhaul the brand.

7   In other initiatives announced on Wednesday, Mars unveiled a $2m investment in culinary scholarships for aspiring black chefs in partnership with the New York-based civil rights organisation the National Urban League. It is also funding nutritional and education programmes to the tune of $2.5m for students in Greenville, Mississippi, the majority African-American city where the rice brand has been produced for more than 40 years, and has set a goal of boosting the ranks of racial minorities in US management positions from 20% to 40%.

Bottle *of Mrs. Butterworth's syrup. Mrs. Butterworth and Cream of Wheat are the latest brands reckoning with racially charged logos.* | PHOTO: *Picture Alliance*

0-2   **REVAMP** Neugestaltung; s.w.u. **revamped** (͵-'-) neu gestaltet — **stereotyping** (ˈsteriətaɪpɪŋ) Stereotypisierung — **branding** Markenimage — **out of step with the times** nicht mehr zeitgemäß — **imagery** (ˈɪmɪdʒəri) Bilder — **bearing** h.: mit — **inequity** (ɪˈnekwɪti) Ungerechtigkeit; Ungleichheit — **to be associated with s.th.** (əˈsəʊsieɪtɪd) mit etw. in Verbindung gebracht werden; s.w.u. **associate** (əˈsəʊʃiət) Mitarbeiter(in)

3-4   **stakeholder** Projektbeteiligte(r) — **executive** (ɪgˈzekjətɪv) Führungskraft — **face** h.: Werbegesicht — **to commit o.s. to s.th.** s. zu etw. entschließen — **to lead s.o. to do s.th.** jdn. zu etw. bewegen — **ripple effect** Welleneffekt; h.: Folge — **to be sparked by s.th.** durch etw. ausgelöst werden

5-6   **syrup** (ˈsɪrəp) Sirup — **character** h.: Werbefigur — **minstrel show** (ˈmɪnstrəl) Aufführung, bei der Schwarze auf stereotypisierende Weise dargestellt werden — **as a reference to** in Bezug auf — **to pledge s.th.** etw. versprechen — **to overhaul** (əʊvəˈhɔːl) überholen; h.: modernisieren

7   **to unveil** (ʌnˈveɪl) bekannt geben — **culinary** (ˈkʌlɪnəri) kulinarisch — **scholarship** (ˈskɒləʃɪp) Stipendium — **aspiring** (əˈspaɪərɪŋ) aufstrebend — **civil rights organisation** Bürgerrechtsorganisation — **to fund** finanzieren — **nutritional** (njuːˈtrɪʃənəl) Ernährungs- — **to the tune of** in Höhe von — **majority** (məˈdʒɒrəti) mehrheitlich — **ranks** Reihen; h.: Anteil — **minority** (maɪˈnɒrəti) Minderheit

Why It Matters When Black Lives Matter Clothing Is Banned

FASHION

The controversy around BLM fashion highlights the systemic racism that the movement is trying to change, writes Priya Elan.

1 FORMULA ONE has banned drivers from wearing clothing bearing messages while performing official duties. The decision came after Lewis Hamilton wore a top at the Tuscan Grand Prix on 13 September that said, "Arrest the cops who killed Breonna Taylor."

2 Since March, celebrities have not shied away from wearing clothing in support of Black Lives Matter (BLM) at high-profile events – but not without a backlash. The Japanese tennis player Naomi Osaka was told to "keep politics out of sport" when she brought seven face masks with the names of different victims of police brutality to the US Open. Almost 2,000 people complained to Ofcom – which has yet to decide whether to investigate – about the BLM necklace worn by Alesha Dixon on *Britain's Got Talent*.

3 The framing of these moments as radical and political rather than sincere and teachable has raised other questions, such as: are black lives allowed to matter in public spaces – public spaces that are normally the home of white privilege?

4 This framing reaffirms the status quo of systemic racism. The fashion historian Darnell-Jamal Lisby says BLM clothes are perceived as threatening because they "shake the belief that conditioned the world to believe that white people are superior". He says they "disrupt a system that privileges those who benefited from the oppression of black people". As such, the wearing of BLM clothing is suppressed (as in the case of Hamilton) or heavily criticised (as Dixon experienced).

Japanese tennis player *Naomi Osaka in September 2020.*
| PHOTO: *Picture Alliance*

5 Last month's Emmys were especially powerful not only because of the number of celebrities wearing BLM clothes but also because the intimate nature of the ceremony (with nominees filmed at home) made their clothes feel more personal than if they were on a red carpet.

6 Sterling K Brown of *This Is Us* wore a dinner jacket over a T-shirt emblazoned with a BLM logo and a black power fist. Yvonne Orji, best known for *Insecure*, had the fist shaved into her hair. *Killing Eve's* Sandra Oh wore a beautiful purple jacket with "Black lives are precious" written on it in Korean.

7 The T-shirt worn by the *Watchmen* writer Damon Lindelof was affecting, too. It bore the words "Remember Tulsa '21", which referenced the 1921 Tulsa massacre, in which as many as 300 black residents of the city in Oklahoma were killed by white mobs. *The Good Place* star William Jackson Harper wore a "Good trouble" T-shirt in honour of the late civil rights leader John Lewis. Regina King

---

0–1 **CONTROVERSY** (ˈkɒntrəvɜːsi) Streit; Kontroverse — **systemic racism** institutioneller Rassismus — **movement** Bewegung — **to bear s.th.** (fig) etw. tragen — **Tuscan Grand Prix** Großer Preis der Toskana
2–3 **to shy away from s.th.** s. vor etw. scheuen — **high-profile** hochkarätig — **backlash** Gegenreaktion — **police brutality** polizeiliche Übergriffe — **framing** Darstellung — **sincere** (sɪnˈsɪə) aufrichtig — **teachable** (ˈtiːtʃəbəl) lehrreich — **home** h.: Domäne — **white privilege** (ˈprɪvəlɪdʒ) Privilegien Weißer; s.w.u. **to privilege** bevorzugen
4 **to reaffirm** (ˌriːəˈfɜːm) bekräftigen — **fashion historian** Modehistoriker(in) — **to be perceived as s.th.** (pəˈsiːvd) als etw. wahrgenommen werden — **threatening** (ˈθretənɪŋ) bedrohlich — **to shake** (fig) erschüttern — **to condition** konditionieren — **superior** überlegen — **oppression** Unterdrückung — **to suppress** (səˈpres) unterdrücken
5–6 **intimate** (ˈɪntɪmət) intim; vertraulich — **nominee** Kandidat(in) — *This Is Us* dt. Titel: *This Is Us – Das ist Leben* — **dinner jacket** Smoking — **to be emblazoned on s.th.** (ɪmˈbleɪzənd) auf etw. prangen — **fist** Faust
7 *Watchmen* dt. Titel: *Watchmen – Die Wächter* — **affecting** bewegend — **to reference s.th.** s. auf etw. beziehen — **as many as** bis zu — **late** verstorben — **civil rights** Bürgerrechte — **respectively** (rɪˈspektɪvli) beziehungsweise — **to honour s.o.** (ˈɒnə) jdn. würdigen
8 **stylist duo** Stylisten-Duo — **empathy** (ˈempəθi) Empathie — **nurture** (ˈnɜːtʃə) Fürsorge; Geborgenheit — **in light of** angesichts — **grand jury** Anklagejury — **sobering** ernüchternd — **reminder** Erinnerung — **injustice** (ɪnˈdʒʌstɪs) Ungerechtigkeit
9–10 **cognisant** (ˈkɒgnɪzənt) bewusst — **more than ever** mehr denn je — **outward** äußerlich; s.w.u. **inward** innerlich — **paddock** Fahrerlager — **podium** Siegerpodest

and Uzo Aduba, who won awards for *Watchmen* and *Mrs America* respectively, wore shirts that honoured Breonna Taylor.

8 "As Nina Simone once said: 'It is the duty of an artist to reflect the times,'" said the stylist duo Wayman Bannerman and Micah McDonald in an email. They worked on King's outfit: "We chose pink as it is the colour of love and empathy. It is a colour of emotion and nurture." In light of a grand jury's decision not to charge officers directly with killing Taylor, the outfits are a sobering reminder of police injustice.

9 Incidents such as a school district in Ohio banning BLM and other slogan T-shirts for being "controversial" show that the role of the celebrity wearing BLM clothes is as important now as it was six months ago. "Being cognisant of the times is important now more than ever," said Bannerman and McDonald. "Clothing is an outward expression of inward emotion."

10 The F1 has responded saying: "Lewis can wear his BLM T-shirt in the paddock and before the race, but like any driver, it has never been allowed on the podium."

A Black Man Forgave the White Cop Who Killed His Brother. Some African Americans Don't Like It

FORGIVING Beyond the spiritual aspect of forgiving is a cultural phenomenon that has shaped who we are as African Americans, says Dahleen Glanton.

1 IT IS HARD for many African Americans to understand why a black man would embrace the white cop who had been convicted of killing his brother. When they look at the photo of Brandt Jean hugging former Dallas police Officer Amber Guyger, they wonder how he could have been so forgiving. Police officers and black men are supposed to be archenemies. Didn't Jean realize that?

2 Speaking during the sentencing phase of the trial, barely able to keep his composure, Jean laid out feelings he had not previously expressed even to his family. "I don't even want you to go to jail," he said. "I want the best for you. ... The best would be giving your life to Christ." Then he asked Judge Tammy Kemp if he could step down and give Guyger a hug. He did, and Guyger rushed into his arms.

3 In a country where law enforcement has been so unforgiving to African Americans, particularly males, how could an 18-year-old black male dole out compassion so generously to a cop whose own text messages revealed her racist thoughts?

4 Perhaps it was for the same reason the African-American judge embraced Guyger at the end of the trial, too. And for the same reason a black female bailiff was seen stroking Guyger's blonde hair after she was found guilty of murder. And for the same reason some family members forgave white supremacist Dylann Roof for shooting up a prayer meeting at Emanuel African Methodist Episcopal Church in Charleston, South Carolina, killing nine people.

5 Maybe it is the mistaken and self-deprecating belief some black people have that they are responsible for white people's racism. This subconscious idea suggests that black people can change the behavior of white people by doing better themselves. If blacks can somehow show that they are worthy of being appreciated and respected, then whites will accept them. And if blacks can demonstrate that they are willing to forgive racists for the hurt they've caused, then racists will willingly become less racist.

6 Of course, many black people will say they forgive because it is what Christianity requires of them. They will say it is because God would not want them to carry the anger around for the rest of their lives. And in exchange for their forgiveness, they often will offer a Bible. ⮢

⁰⁻² **PHENOMENON** (fə'nɒmɪnən) Phänomen — **to shape s.o./s.th.** (fig) jdn./etw. prägen — **to embrace s.o.** (ɪm'breɪs) jdn. umarmen — **to convict s.o.** (-'-) jdn. verurteilen — **forgiving** versöhnlich; s.w.u. **unforgiving** gnadenlos — **archenemy** (ˌɑːtʃ'enəmi) Erzfeind(in) — **sentencing phase** Urteilsverkündung — **to keep one's composure** (kəm'pəʊʒə) die Fassung bewahren — **to lay out** h.: offenlegen

³⁻⁵ **law enforcement** (ɪn'fɔːsmənt) Polizei — **to dole out** austeilen; h.: zuteilwerden lassen — **compassion** Mitgefühl — **bailiff** Gerichtsdiener(in) — **white supremacist** (suː'preməsɪst) Neonazi; Anhänger(in) der Ideologie von der vermeintlichen Überlegenheit Weißer — **to shoot up** das Feuer eröffnen — **prayer meeting** Bibelandacht — **mistaken** irrtümlich — **self-deprecating** (ˌ-'deprəkeɪtɪŋ) s. selbst herabsetzend — **subconscious** (ˌsʌb'kɒnʃəs) unbewusst — **to be worthy of s.th.** ('wɜːði) etw. würdig sein

⁶⁻⁷ **Christianity** (ˌkrɪsti'ænəti) der christliche Glaube — **to carry s.th. around** etw. mit s. herumtragen — **forgiveness** Vergebung —

7 No one can argue with how a person chooses to cope with tragedy. Nor is it up to anyone to decide how survivors should come to terms with their grief. And it is certainly not our place to question their relationship with God. But beyond the spiritual aspect of forgiving with such great magnitude is a cultural phenomenon that has shaped who we are as African Americans from the moment we entered this country enslaved. It is what sustained us through slavery, through decades of lynchings and cross burnings, and through police killings, economic inequities, and social injustices.

8 It is the belief that, in spite of the racial atrocities inflicted on blacks, even those who seem to hate us deserve a chance for redemption. And it is our job to help them find it. Many whites have been more than happy to sit back and allow black people to do all the redemptive work.

9 When they consider Brandt Jean's hug, they see courage. They admire him for being able to let bygones be bygones. They hold him up as a model for how blacks should respond to adversity, pain, and anger. They are at ease with their feelings because Jean gave them permission to remain in their comfort zone.

10 These attitudes, however, are fading as a younger generation takes over the mantle. Younger blacks are not as patient as their parents and grandparents were, and they are less willing to take the responsibility of teaching white people what it means to be black. As far as they are concerned, anybody who wants to know the facts about blacks in America must take it upon themselves to find out.

11 And many younger whites, as a result, are less dependent on African Americans to teach them about the black experience. They proactively seek information because they know that understanding America's racial history is crucial to its future.

12 When young people gathered outside the courthouse in Guyger's case to await the verdict, the crowd was diverse. They felt collectively that Guyger's 10-year prison sentence for shooting a man in his own home because she entered the wrong apartment was a slap in the face. And they said so in angry chants outside the courthouse. They were aware that the light sentence is reflective of the inequities of the judicial system, which historically has applied harsher sentences to African Americans than to whites who committed similar crimes. …

13 They understood that Guyger's decision to shoot Botham Jean to death because she believed that he was an intruder is a symptom of much bigger problems with race that plague police departments across the country. They are problems that have led to far too many deaths of black men who should not have been killed.

14 We don't know who Guyger really is in her heart. The best we can do is surmise from what she has shown us. In text messages released during the sentencing, Guyger made several racist remarks, and in one, she appeared to acknowledge that she is racist.

15 The idea that blacks can "fix" white people is flawed. What it fails to recognize is that nobody can fix anybody. Each of us has the power to change who we are if we want to change. The problem with racists, though, is that they often don't realize that they need to be fixed. Or if they do, they don't want to be fixed.

---

to come to terms with s.th. etw. verarbeiten — **it is not our place** es steht uns nicht zu — **magnitude** ('mægnɪtʃuːd) Ausmaß; Größe — **enslaved** (ɪn'sleɪvd) versklavt — **to sustain** Kraft geben — **lynching** ('lɪntʃɪŋ) Lynchmord — **cross burning** Kreuzverbrennung (als Symbol des Ku-Klux-Klan) — **inequity** (ɪ'nekwɪti) Ungleichheit — **injustice** (ɪn'dʒʌstɪs) Ungerechtigkeit

8–10 **atrocity** (ə'trɒsəti) Gräueltat — **to inflict s.th. on s.o.** jdm. etw. zufügen — **redemption** Erlösung; s.w.u. **redemptive** (rɪ'demptɪv) Erlösungs- — **to sit back** (fig) s. zurücklehnen — **to let bygones be bygones** ('baɪɡɒnz) die Vergangenheit ruhen lassen — **to hold s.o. up as a model** jdn. als Vorbild hinstellen — **adversity** (əd'vɜːsəti) Widrigkeit — **to give permission** die Erlaubnis geben — **to fade** verblassen; schwinden — **to take over the mantle** die Führung übernehmen — **to take s.th. upon o.s.** etw. selbst in die Hand nehmen

11–12 **proactively** (ˌ-'æktɪvli) proaktiv — **crucial** ('kruːʃəl) entscheidend — **courthouse** Gerichtsgebäude — **to await s.th.** (ə'weɪt) auf etw. warten — **verdict** Urteil — **collectively** (kə'lektɪvli) allesamt — **a slap in the face** (fig) ein Schlag ins Gesicht — **chant** h.: Sprechchor — **to be reflective of s.th.** (rɪ'flektɪv) etw. widerspiegeln — **judicial system** (dʒuː'dɪʃəl) Justizsystem — **historically** h.: in der Vergangenheit — **to apply** h.: verhängen — **harsh** hart

13–15 **intruder** (ɪn'truːdə) Eindringling — **to plague** (pleɪɡ) (fig) plagen — **in one's heart** tief im Innersten — **to surmise** (sə'maɪz) vermuten — **to release** h.: veröffentlichen — **to acknowledge s.th.** (ək'nɒlɪdʒ) etw. eingestehen — **to fix s.o.** h.: jdn. e-s Besseren belehren — **flawed** (flɔːd) fehlerhaft

White Privilege – and the American Caste System – Was on Display During the Insurrection

STORMING OF THE CAPITOL
Black men and women likely would have been shot down for taking over the preeminent symbol of American democracy, says Dahleen Glanton.

1 WHEN THE insurrection on Capitol Hill was over, midlife Black men in navy blue custodial uniforms cleaned up the mess. The viral video of the janitors sweeping debris from the hallway was as telling as any image of the day. It told a story beyond the photos of white people scaling the exterior walls of the Capitol, breaking windows to gain entry, or the man lounging in the House speaker's office chair with his feet propped upon her desk.

2 It was a resignation without a word spoken. As is often the case, Black people were left to clean up the mess, this time left by whites who stormed the Capitol in an attempt to force Congress to invalidate Black votes.

3 There is one thing on which most of us can agree regarding the insurrection. White rioters were treated differently than African Americans. Black men – and women – likely would have been shot down for taking over this sacred building, the preeminent symbol of American democracy. But white people, for the most part, were allowed to roam freely.

4 We should consider it progress that so many white people realize that a much harsher system of justice is applied to African Americans. Or perhaps what is new is that some white people are now quicker to say it publicly. But saying it out loud is not enough. We must come together as a nation to force the justice system into balance. However, we cannot begin to figure out how to do that until we understand why it always has been so lopsided.

Workers remove *damaged furniture in the Capitol building a day after the riots of January 6, 2021.*
| Photo: *Getty Images*

5 It is easy to attribute everything that happens unfairly to African Americans to racism. Racism has become a catchall phrase for anything in which the majority race receives unwarranted precedence over the minority race. Often, it is indeed racism, but that is not always the entire story.

6 My friend Isabel Wilkerson, whom I met years ago when she was a national correspondent for *The New York Times* based in Chicago, suggests that the injustice we most often see is something more complex. It is the adherence to a caste system that is as much a part of America's DNA as it was in Nazi Germany and today in India.

7 Her book, *Caste: The Origins of Our Discontents*, provides insight into the inner workings of America's caste system. In her book, Wilkerson describes America's caste system as a social hierarchy that was established centuries ago "based upon ⊃

---

0 **CASTE SYSTEM** (kɑːst) Kastensystem; s.w.u. **casteism** Kastendenken — **to be on display** offen zur Schau stellen — **insurrection** (ˌɪnsərˈekʃən) Aufstand; Aufruhr — **to take over** Besitz ergreifen — **preeminent** (priˈemənənt) herausragend

1 **midlife** im mittleren Alter — **custodial uniform** (kʌsˈtəʊdiəl) Hausmeisteruniform — **janitor** (ˈdʒænɪtə) Hausmeister(in); s.w.u. **janitorial** (dʒænɪˈtɔːriəl) Hausmeister- — **debris** (ˈdebriː) Trümmer — **hallway** Flur — **telling** aufschlussreich — **to scale** erklimmen — **exterior wall** Außenwand — **to lounge** (laʊndʒ) h.: lungern — **House speaker** Sprecher(in) des US-Repräsentantenhauses — **to prop up one's feet** seine Füße hochlegen

2–4 **as is often the case** wie so oft — **to invalidate s.th.** (ɪnˈvælɪdeɪt) etw. für ungültig erklären — **rioter** (ˈraɪətə) Randalierer(in) — **sacred** (ˈseɪkrɪd) heilig; ehrwürdig — **for the most part** überwiegend — **to roam freely** s. frei bewegen — **harsh** streng — **to force s.th. into balance** etw. ins Gleichgewicht rücken — **lopsided** (ˌ-ˈ--) (fig) einseitig

5–6 **to attribute** (əˈtrɪbjuːt) zuschreiben — **catchall phrase** (ˈkætʃɔːl) Sammelbegriff — **unwarranted** (ʌnˈwɒrəntɪd) ungerechtfertigt — **precedence** (ˈpresɪdəns) Vorrang — **correspondent** Korrespondent(in) — **injustice** Unrecht — **adherence** (ədˈhɪərəns) Festhalten; s.w.wu. **to adhere to s.th.** an etw. festhalten — **as much … as** ebenso … wie — **DNA** (fig) Identität

7 **discontent** (ˌdɪskənˈtent) Unzufriedenheit — **insight** Einblick — **inner workings** Innenleben —

⤵ what people looked like, an internalized ranking, unspoken, unnamed, unacknowledged by everyday citizens even as they go about their lives adhering to it and acting upon it subconsciously to this day."

8 Caste and race are interwoven in America, she explains, and it can be hard to separate the two. She distinguishes them this way: "Any action or institution that mocks, harms, assumes, or attaches inferiority or stereotype on the basis of the social construct of race can be considered racism," she writes. "Any action or structure that seeks to limit, hold back, or put someone in a defined ranking, seeks to keep someone in their place by elevating or denigrating that person on the basis of their perceived category, can be seen as casteism." Caste is structure, she writes. Caste is ranking. Simply put, caste is about keeping "those on your disfavored rung from gaining on you."

9 It should surprise no one that Black people rank lowest in the caste system and white people comprise the upper caste. So from their perch at the top of the hierarchy, white people are allowed to get away with things that Black people cannot. Their entitlement is widely recognized, even by some in law enforcement.

10 According to Wilkerson, casteism "may flare and reassert itself in times of upheaval and recede in times of relative calm," but it is always there. Let's look at what happened last week through the lens of the caste system. Swarms of white people descended upon Washington demanding that the government return something they believed had been stolen from them, in this case, an election. They had no proof to back it up. Caste does not require it.

11 "Caste is the granting or withholding of respect, status, honor, attention, privileges, resources, benefit of the doubt, and human kindness to someone on the basis of their perceived rank or standing in the hierarchy," Wilkerson writes. Caste reaffirms white people's standing. Even whites at the bottom of the social economic scale could be assured that they held title to something that no one else did – that America has always belonged to them.

12 Finally, there was a president who understood the natural order, and his supporters would go to any lengths to keep him in office. So they burst into the Capitol. It was not trespassing because this building and everything inside belonged to them. They shouted, "Our house! Our house!" …

13 A caste system allows miscarriage of justice. It is not always intentional. It is simply inherent and, most importantly, invisible. According to Wilkerson, its very invisibility is what gives it power and longevity. Perhaps the most unseemly reward granted to those at the top of the hierarchy is entitlement. The caste structure sustains it and everyone, including some at the bottom, accepts it and sometimes, seemingly inexplicably, helps it to thrive.

14 It is common for those in the marginalized castes, Wilkerson writes, to "curry the favor and remain in the good graces of the dominant caste, all of which serves to keep the structure intact." That explains why an Afro-Cuban might accept the leadership of the extremist group, the Proud Boys, and why a sprinkling of Black people always can be found among counter-protesters of Black Lives Matter. It is why a handful of Black people were among those who stormed the Capitol demanding that votes of other Black people in Pennsylvania, Michigan, and Georgia be tossed out as illegitimate.

15 So when the cleaning crew arrived, it was expected that many would be African Americans. Though janitorial work is entirely respectable, certain jobs are reserved for those at the bottom of the hierarchy. Cleaning up after those at the top reflects the internal ranking within America. It is required under a system built on caste.

---

internalized (ɪn'tɜːnəlaɪzd) verinnerlicht — **unacknowledged** (ʌnək'nɒlɪdʒd) uneingestanden — **everyday citizen** Durchschnittsbürger(in) — **to go about one's life doing s.th.** sein Leben damit verbringen, etw. zu tun — **to act upon s.th.** nach etw. handeln — **subconsciously** (ˌsʌb'kɒnʃəsli) unbewusst — **to this day** bis heute
8   **interwoven** (fig) verflochten — **to mock** verspotten — **to assume** (ə'sjuːm) unterstellen — **to attach** zuschreiben — **inferiority** (ɪnˌfɪəri'ɒrəti) Minderwertigkeit — **social construct** soziales Konstrukt — **to seek s.th.** auf etw. abzielen — **to keep s.o. in their place** jdn. in die Schranken weisen — **to elevate s.o.** ('elɪveɪt) jdn. aufwerten — **to denigrate s.o.** ('denɪgreɪt) jdn. abwerten — **perceived** (pə'siːvd) vermeintlich — **simply put** einfach ausgedrückt — **disfavored** (dɪs'feɪvəd) benachteiligt — **rung** (fig) Sprosse — **to gain on s.o.** jdn. einholen
9   **to comprise s.th.** etw. bilden — **perch** Hochsitz; h.: Platz — **entitlement** (ɪn'taɪtəlmənt) Anspruch — **law enforcement** (ɪn'fɔːsmənt) Polizei
10   **to flare** (fig) aufflammen — **to reassert o.s.** (ˌriːə'sɜːt) s. wieder durchsetzen — **in times of upheaval** (ʌp'hiːvəl) in Umbruchzeiten — **to recede** (rɪ'siːd) (fig) zurückgehen — **calm** Ruhe — **to look at s.th. through the lens of s.th.** etw. vor dem Hintergrund von etw. betrachten — **swarm** (swɔːm) Schwarm; Horde — **to descend on s.o./s.th.** (dɪ'send) über jdn./etw. hereinbrechen — **to back s.th. up** etw. belegen
11–12 **to withhold** vorenthalten — **benefit of the doubt** Vertrauensbonus — **standing** Position — **to reaffirm** (ˌriːə'fɜːm) erneut bekräftigen — **at the bottom of the scale** am unteren Ende der Skala — **to hold title to s.th.** ein Anrecht auf etw. haben — **to go to any lengths** (leŋθ) alle Hebel in Bewegung setzen — **to keep s.o. in office** jdn. im Amt halten — **trespassing** ('trespəsɪŋ) Hausfriedensbruch
13   **miscarriage of justice** ('mɪsˌkærɪdʒ) Justizirrtum — **intentional** beabsichtigt — **inherent** (ɪn'herənt) innewohnend — **its very** gerade seine — **invisibility** (ɪnˌvɪzə'bɪləti) Unsichtbarkeit — **longevity** (lɒn'dʒevəti) Langlebigkeit; Dauerhaftigkeit — **unseemly** ungebührlich — **reward** Belohnung — **to sustain** aufrechterhalten — **seemingly** scheinbar — **inexplicably** (ˌɪnɪk'splɪkəbli) unerklärlicherweise — **to thrive** (θraɪv) (fig) gedeihen
14–15 **marginalized** ('mɑːdʒɪnəlaɪzd) marginalisiert; an den Rand gedrängt — **to curry favor** ('kʌri) s. anbiedern — **to remain in s.o.'s good graces** s. jds. Gunst sichern — **to serve to do s.th.** dazu dienen, etw. zu tun — **Afro-Cuban** Afrokubaner(in) — **a sprinkling of** h.: e-e Handvoll — **counterprotester** Gegendemonstrant(in) — **to toss out** verwerfen — **illegitimate** (ˌɪlɪ'dʒɪtəmət) unrechtmäßig

'Black Lives Matter' Risks Becoming an Empty Slogan

SLOGAN There are three powerful words that do expose discrimination, but you won't find them chanted in the street, says Joseph Harker.

1 IF I HEAR one more white person say "Black Lives Matter," I think my head will explode. The slogan, powerful when first popularised by black people after the shooting of Trayvon Martin in 2012 in the US, has now become so ubiquitous as to have lost almost all meaning. A way for people to endlessly repeat "I hate racism" while doing nothing to actually stop it. …

2 Even racists hate racism. That's why they're always looking for ways to excuse what they do. "It's not my fault – black people are just a bit more criminal than white people." "I'm not being racist – it's just that a lot of Muslims are terrorists." "I'd love to recruit a black person – it's just that they're not quite the right fit for this role."

3 "It's just that …" You won't find this chanted in a city square by thousands of protesters, but these are probably the three most powerful words in the history of institutional racism. They're the words people say in private – or don't say – when they're making the decisions that really matter. They are the words that determine whether someone gets that job or that business contract or that university place or that rented room.

4 Over the past few days, I've wondered, why now? Why, after all we've known about police brutality against black people, are people only now saying, en masse, that enough is enough? I think there are two core reasons. First, given the lockdown, there's not a lot else for young people to do. The anger is genuine, but the usual distractions that stop people from turning out have gone. It's the first time in months that young people have been able to be part of a group activity.

5 But the other factor is more fundamental: and that is, white guilt. While black people have raged about the shootings and asphyxiations, for most white people, there's always been a get-out.

6 "It's just that [those words again] … he was maybe being too aggressive … maybe the officers thought they were under threat … it was a spur-of-the-moment pull of the trigger." It's allowed white people to believe that, though the outcomes were all horrific, a white suspect in the same situation could have suffered the same fate. The George Floyd video crashed through that delusion. A subdued and incapacitated suspect; a knee pushed down on his neck as he pleaded for breath; passers-by screaming for his life as it ebbed away; officer Derek Chauvin blithely ignoring it all, cocksure that he'd face no consequences for his actions; a fellow officer standing guard to prevent anyone coming to Floyd's rescue. For almost nine minutes, many of them after he had passed out. Nine minutes.

7 No white person could believe this could happen to them. That an officer of the law could be so callous, so unconcerned about the life of a white man. That's why, this time, there have been unprecedented numbers of white people declaring their allegiance to the antiracism cause. On the streets, even in the US, most protesters have been white. Though many of these new activists will have only a superficial understanding of race issues, it has to be a positive thing that at last they're starting to notice.

8 This was nowhere more apparent than in Bristol this weekend. If it had been a black-only crowd, would the statue of notorious slave master Edward Colston really have been allowed to topple, let alone be dragged through the streets and dumped in the River Avon? ➔

0–3 **EMPTY** h.: bedeutungslos — **to chant** skandieren — **to popularise** ('pɒpjələraɪz) bekannt machen — **ubiquitous** (juːˈbɪkwɪtəs) allgegenwärtig — **it's just that …** es ist halt so, dass … — **to recruit s.o.** jdn. einstellen — **to not be the right fit** nicht geeignet sein — **protester** Demonstrant(in) — **institutional racism** institutioneller Rassismus — **to determine** (dɪˈtɜːmɪn) h.: entscheiden

4–5 **police brutality** polizeiliche Übergriffe — **only now** erst jetzt — **core reason** Hauptgrund (**core** Kern) — **given** angesichts — **genuine** ('dʒenjuɪn) echt; aufrichtig — **distraction** Ablenkung — **fundamental** grundlegend — **to rage** wüten — **asphyxiation** (əsˌfɪksiˈeɪʃən) Erstickung — **get-out** Ausrede

6 **to be under threat** (θret) bedroht werden — **spur-of-the-moment** (spɜː) kurzschlussartig — **to pull the trigger** den Abzug betätigen — **outcome** Folge — **horrific** (həˈrɪfɪk) verheerend — **to suffer the same fate** das gleiche Schicksal erleiden — **to crash through s.th.** (fig) etw. durchbrechen — **delusion** Illusion — **subdued** (səbˈdjuːd) gebändigt — **incapacitated** (ˌɪnkəˈpæsɪteɪtɪd) bewegungsunfähig — **to plead for s.th.** um etw. flehen — **passer-by** Passant(in) — **to ebb away**; s.w.u. **to drain away** dahinschwinden — **blithely** ('blaɪðli) unbekümmert — **cocksure** (ˌkɒkˈʃɔː) (coll) vollkommen sicher — **to stand guard** Wache stehen — **to come to s.o.'s rescue** jdm. zu Hilfe kommen

7 **officer of the law** Gesetzeshüter(in) — **callous** ('kæləs) gefühllos — **unconcerned** (ˌʌnkənˈsɜːnd) gleichgültig — **unprecedented** (ʌnˈpresɪdentɪd) beispiellos — **to declare allegiance to s.th.** (əˈliːdʒəns) s. zu etw. bekennen — **cause** Sache; Anliegen — **superficial** (ˌsuːpəˈfɪʃəl) oberflächlich — **race issue** Rassismusproblem

8–9 **notorious** (nəʊˈtɔːrɪəs) berüchtigt — **slave master** Sklavenhalter — **to topple** (um)stürzen — **let alone** geschweige denn —

9 Many British people were upset at what they saw. And I have some sympathy: mob rule is generally a bad thing and risks getting disastrously out of hand. But what a glorious moment. It's an image that will last years in the memory, as the moment that people in one English city said the ritual humiliation of black lives was no longer acceptable. You can say "Black Lives Matter" a million times, but it will change nothing. This action changed things.

10 When I saw Floyd's life drain slowly away, I wondered why so little had changed since the Black Lives Matter movement swept across the US in 2014. Surely all US police officers should know they will be held accountable for any transgressions, especially when caught on camera?

11 There are 18,000 separate police forces in the US. In the UK there are 43. If we're going to bring about change, we need to find a way to get into them all, change them all, and make those changes stick. It won't be by simply calling for more black police officers. That's been tried before, and any change is glacially slow. It won't be just by rooting out "bad apples": a system that allows them in unchecked in the first place is already rotten to the core. It won't simply be by giving all officers "diversity training": a couple of weeks on the streets after completing such a course, and they're back in the old routine, acting on the instincts and stereotypes.

12 On the day of the first major UK Black Lives Matter protest last Wednesday, the Metropolitan police commissioner, Cressida Dick, was giving evidence to the London assembly. She was talking, coincidentally, about the disproportionate number of fines handed out to black people during the coronavirus lockdown – double the rate for white people.

13 This, she explained, was partly because more officers have been operating in high-crime areas. To which the response must be, what has the lockdown got to do with high-crime areas? It's just another way in which black people (more likely to live in poorer areas, which are more likely to have higher crime rates) continue to be disproportionately targeted by the police. …

14 This is where leadership really counts: the day-to-day decisions, at the most senior levels, that affect thousands of lives. To make lasting change, we ultimately have to get off the streets and into the rooms where these decision-makers operate.

15 Barack Obama has set out an intelligent long-term plan which involves working locally with US mayors, district attorneys, and local police chiefs. In the UK, we have to be equally thoughtful – so that every single officer, every single business chief, every head of every institution thinks every single day about the need to eradicate racism and bias. Black Lives Matter is a catchy slogan. But right now, action is what really matters.

---

to dump wegwerfen — **mob rule** Pöbelherrschaft — **to get out of hand** außer Kontrolle geraten — **disastrously** (drˈzɑːstrəsli) katastrophal — **glorious** glorreich — **ritual** (ˈrɪtʃuəl) rituell — **humiliation** (hjuːˌmɪliˈeɪʃən) Demütigung

10   **movement** Bewegung — **to sweep across s.th.** über etw. hinwegfegen — **to hold s.o. accountable** (əˈkaʊntəbəl) jdn. zur Rechenschaft ziehen — **transgression** (trænzˈgreʃən) Verstoß — **to catch s.th. on camera** mit der Kamera festhalten; filmen

11   **to bring s.th. about** etw. bewirken — **to make s.th. stick** etw. konsequent durchsetzen — **to call for s.th.** etw. fordern — **glacially slow** (ˈgleɪsiəli) extrem langsam (**glacier** Gletscher) — **to root out** entwurzeln; h.: entfernen — **bad apples** (fig) schwarze Schafe — **unchecked** unkontrolliert — **rotten to the core** h.: (fig) durch und durch verdorben — **diversity training** Diversitätsschulung — **to act on s.th.** nach etw. handeln

12–13 **police commissioner** (kəˈmɪʃənə) Chef(in) der Polizeibehörde — **to give evidence** (ˈevɪdəns) aussagen — **London assembly** Legislativbehörde für Greater London — **coincidentally** (kəʊˌɪnsɪˈdentəli) zufällig — **disproportionate** (ˌdɪsprəˈpɔːʃənət) unverhältnismäßig — **to operate** (ˈɒpəreɪt) im Einsatz sein; s.w.u. agieren — **high-crime area** Gegend mit hoher Kriminalität; s.w.u. **crime rate** Kriminalitätsrate — **to target s.o./s.th.** jdn./etw. ins Visier nehmen

14–15 **day-to-day** tagtäglich — **lasting** dauerhaft — **ultimately** (ˈʌltɪmətli) letztlich — **district attorney** Bezirksstaatsanwalt(-anwältin) — **equally** (ˈiːkwəli) ebenso — **to eradicate s.th.** (ɪˈrædɪkeɪt) etw. ausmerzen — **bias** (ˈbaɪəs) Vorurteil — **catchy** eingängig

Supporters *of US President Donald Trump protest inside the US Capitol on January 6, 2021.* | PHOTO: *Getty Images*

BLM Protestors Are the Real American Patriots

PATRIOTISM The Black Lives Matter movement is deeply committed to American values, says Joshua J. Kassner.

1 RESPONSES to and analyses of the Jan. 6 seditious attack on the nation's capital by a mob of Donald Trump's supporters have been wide ranging. Of particular significance has been the outcry over the disparity between the police response to the pro-Trump rioters and their response to the largely peaceful Black Lives Matter protests this past summer.

2 One can't escape the racial overtones laid bare by this juxtaposition. There is, however, an additional difference between BLM and Trump's insurrectionists to be noted: It is the former, not the latter, who are patriots committed to American values.

3 This may not be obvious to some. One might look at the fact that the BLM movement is grounded in a claim that racial injustice is woven into the fabric of our social, political, and economic systems and wonder how one can object to the system yet be committed to the values it is meant to instantiate. Answering this question is the key to understanding how deeply committed the BLM movement is to American values.

4 To explain, the BLM movement is based on the proposition that our institutions have, for too many and for too long, failed to live up to their promise. The BLM movement merely demands that this promise be fulfilled. The BLM movement leans on our shared political values – liberty, equality of opportunity, and the rule of law – to point out that our collective political project is not finished.

5 One need not agree with their interpretation of these values or the impact that they claim these values ought to have (though I do) to recognize that the BLM project is one that seeks to perfect the American project by demanding that our shared values are made manifest for all. BLM demands that America lives up to its aspirations. ➐

0–1 **PROTESTER** (prəˈtestə) Demonstrant(in) — **patriot** (ˈpætriət) Patriot(in) — **movement** Bewegung — **to be committed to s.th.** etw. verpflichtet sein — **seditious** (sɪˈdɪʃəs) aufrührerisch — **wide ranging** umfassend — **significance** (sɪɡˈnɪfɪkəns) Bedeutung — **outcry** (ˈ--) (fig) Aufschrei — **disparity** Diskrepanz — **rioter** (ˈraɪətə) Randalierer(in)
2–3 **to escape s.th.** s. etw. entziehen — **overtone** (fig) Unterton — **to lay bare** offenbaren — **juxtaposition** (ˌdʒʌkstəpəˈzɪʃən) Gegenüberstellung — **insurrectionist** (ˌɪnsəˈrekʃənɪst) Aufrührer(in) — **to be grounded in s.th.** auf etw. beruhen — **claim** Behauptung — **injustice** (ɪnˈdʒʌstɪs) Ungerechtigkeit — **to be woven into s.th.** mit etw. verwoben sein — **fabric** (ˈfæbrɪk) Gefüge — **to instantiate** (ɪnˈstænʃieɪt) repräsentieren
4–5 **proposition** These — **to live up to s.th.** etw. gerecht werden — **to fulfill** erfüllen — **to lean on s.th.** (fig) s. auf etw. stützen — **equality of opportunity** (iˈkwɒləti) Chancengleichheit — **rule of law** Rechtsstaatlichkeit — **collective** gemeinsam — **to seek s.th.** etw. anstreben — **to perfect** (-ˈ-) vollenden; vervollkommnen — **to make manifest** (ˈmænɪfest) manifestieren — **aspiration** Anspruch

6 The same cannot be said for those who stormed the Capitol building on Jan. 6. In fact, despite their rhetorical appeals to 1776 and their ostensive belief in the patriotic nature of their actions, the fact that the flags they flew were dominated by Trump campaign flags and included Confederate flags and banners of white supremacist gangs should be indication enough of where their loyalties lie.

7 If we think of what their actions tell us, they violently stormed and looted our nation's capital, seeking to overturn an election through forceful and unlawful means. In an effort to deny the will of the American people, they were implicitly denying the political equality of their fellow citizens, and they were undermining our political freedom, not defending it.

8 I should note that, though I may find many of the views held by Trump's supporters to be misguided if not wrong, those who chose not to take part in the storming of the Capitol building are not the object of this critique. Nothing I say here applies to those who were peacefully exercising their right to free expression. Even if I disagree with you, I respect your right to peacefully express your views.

9 For those who did choose the path of violence, some may claim that the intentions of these insurrectionists were, in fact, in line with the American commitment to democracy and freedom, that they were seeking to defend our democratic way of life. It is just that they have been fed a steady diet of lies and misinformation, and as a consequence, we can't hold them accountable for their ignorance or their actions.

10 For the sake of argument, I will set aside my belief that the willful ignorance upon which this proposition relies is no excuse and instead focus on the claim on its own terms.

11 With this caveat noted, the values of our democratic republic include respect for the rule of law and a commitment to the proposition that every individual deserves equal respect within our legal and political processes.

12 In practice, this means that we respect the results of our elections and challenge them through the courts. It is our commitment to these institutions that allows a people as diverse as ours to live together and govern ourselves. To ignore the unanimous decisions of courts across this country and then try to overturn our election through force is an act of tyranny and not democracy, no matter what cloak you try to hide beneath.

13 I hope that in the aftermath of this crisis, we join BLM in the project of perfecting our republic, of living out the shared values that make our collective political life possible.

---

6   **to storm** erstürmen — **rhetorical** rhetorisch — **appeal** Appell — **ostensive** (ɒˈstensɪv) scheinbar — **to fly** h.: schwenken — **campaign** Wahlkampf — **Confederate flag** (kənˈfedərət) Konföderiertenflagge — **banner** Spruchband — **white supremacist** (suːˈpreməsɪst) Neonazi; Anhänger(in) der Ideologie von der vermeintlichen Überlegenheit Weißer — **indication** Indiz

7–8   **to loot** plündern — **to overturn** kippen — **forceful** gewaltsam — **unlawful** (ʌnˈlɔːfəl) unrechtmäßig — **the will of the people** der Volkswille — **implicitly** (ɪmˈplɪsɪtli) implizit — **to undermine s.th.** (fig) etw. untergraben — **to hold a view** e-e Ansicht vertreten — **misguided** (ˌ-ˈɡaɪdɪd) fehlgeleitet — **object** (fig) Gegenstand — **critique** (krɪˈtiːk) Kritik — **to excercise** ausüben

9–10   **to be in line with s.th.** mit etw. übereinstimmen — **to feed s.o. a diet of s.th.** (fig) jdm. etw. einflößen — **misinformation** Fehlinformationen — **as a consequence** (ˈkɒnsɪkwəns) infolgedessen — **to hold s.o. accountable** (əˈkaʊntəbəl) jdn. zur Verantwortung ziehen — **ignorance** (ˈɪɡnərəns) Unwissenheit — **for the sake of …** um … willen — **to set aside s.th.** etw. beiseitelassen — **willful** vorsätzlich

11–13   **caveat** (ˈkæviæt) Vorbehalt — **to challenge** h.: anfechten — **unanimous** (juːˈnænɪməs) einhellig — **tyranny** (ˈtɪrəni) Tyrannei — **cloak** (fig) Deckmantel — **in the aftermath of s.th.** nach etw. — **to live out** ausleben

Photo: Getty Images

On June 19, 2020, *thousands of New Yorkers took to the streets for a third straight week to commemorate Juneteenth, the June 19 date in 1865 that marks the end of slavery in the United States.* | PHOTO: *Picture Alliance*

On May 25, 2021, *BLM protesters gathered in New York City for the one-year anniversary of George Floyd's death.* | PHOTO: *Getty Images*

Activists from *United for Black Lives outside Parliament in London in May 2021. They are protesting against a bill which would grant the police a range of new discretionary powers to shut down protests as well as wider stop and search powers.* | PHOTO: *Getty Images*

New York Police Department *(NYPD) officers detaining a protester during a Black Lives Matter demonstration in New York City in November 2020.* | PHOTO: *Picture Alliance/Reuters*

Homemade protest signs *for people to pick up and use for a protest march in Brooklyn.* | PHOTO: *Getty Images*

Protestors having *a discussion with a commanding officer in Cleveland, Ohio, in September 2020.* | PHOTO: *Picture Alliance*

A protester *in New York on President Donald Trump's 74th birthday on June 14, 2020.* | PHOTO: *Getty Images*

The US women's *football team stands during the national anthem before a friendly match against France in April 2021. The players are wearing t-shirts in support of the Black Lives Matter campaign.* | PHOTO: *Picture Alliance/Reuters*

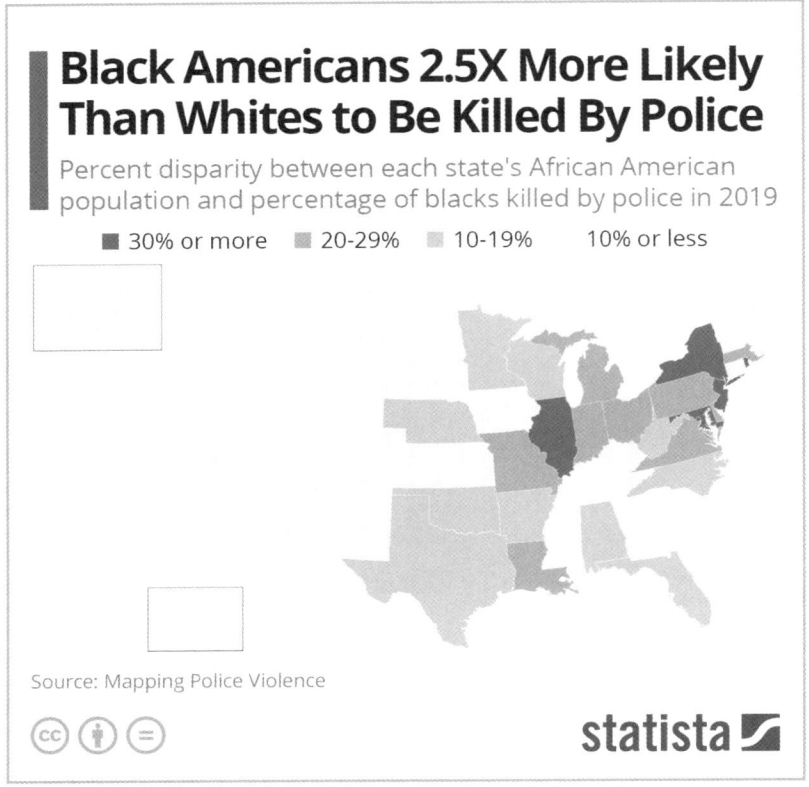

Black Americans 2.5X More Likely Than Whites to Be Killed By Police

Percent disparity between each state's African American population and percentage of blacks killed by police in 2019

■ 30% or more   ■ 20-29%   ■ 10-19%   10% or less

Source: Mapping Police Violence

statista

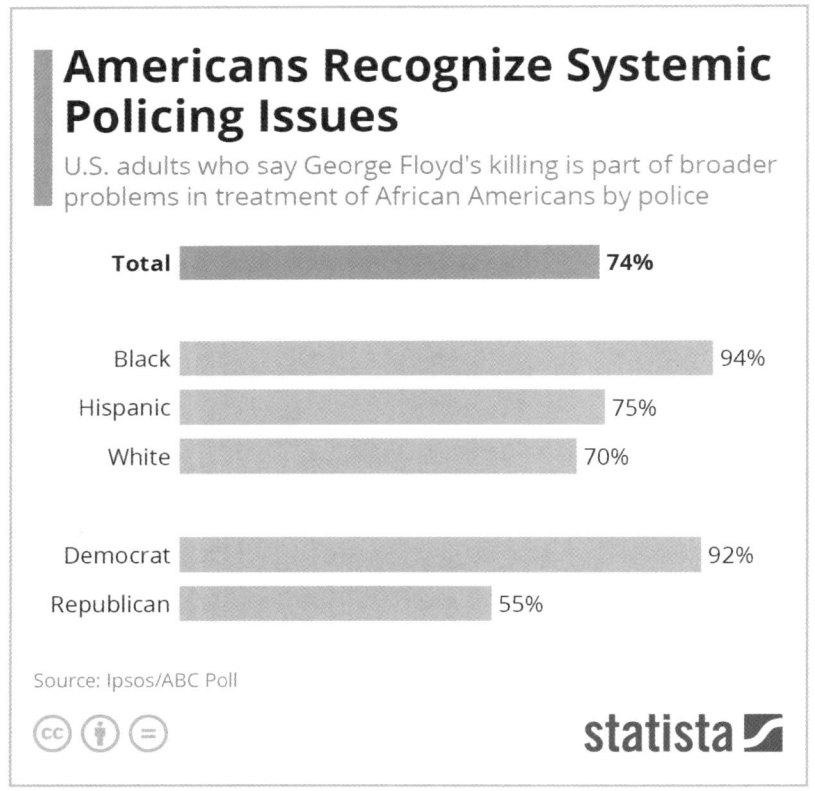

Americans Recognize Systemic Policing Issues

U.S. adults who say George Floyd's killing is part of broader problems in treatment of African Americans by police

Total	74%
Black	94%
Hispanic	75%
White	70%
Democrat	92%
Republican	55%

Source: Ipsos/ABC Poll

statista

| GRAPHICS: *Statista*

The People Killed by U.S. Police in 2020

Breakdown of people killed by police in the United States in 2020

Gender

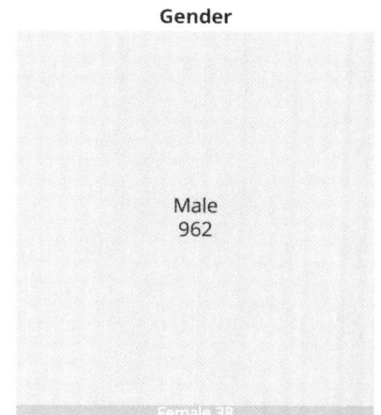

Male
962

Female 38

Race

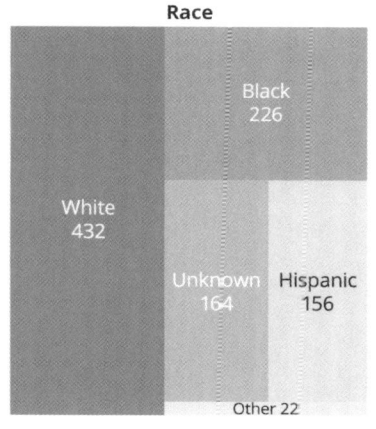

White
432

Black
226

Unknown
164

Hispanic
156

Other 22

Were armed with

Gun
622

Knife
166

Unknown
56

Other Weapon
43

Unarmed
41

Vehicle
47

Toy weapon
25

Source: Washington Post

Higher Rate of Police Force on Black People in Minneapolis

Types of force used by the Minneapolis police and percent share based on ethnicity

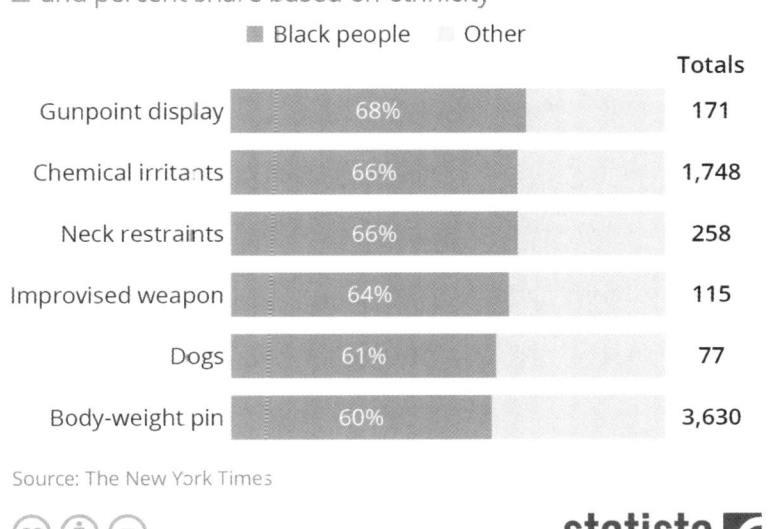

	Black people	Other	Totals
Gunpoint display	68%		171
Chemical irritants	66%		1,748
Neck restraints	66%		258
Improvised weapon	64%		115
Dogs	61%		77
Body-weight pin	60%		3,630

Source: The New York Times

statista ⚊

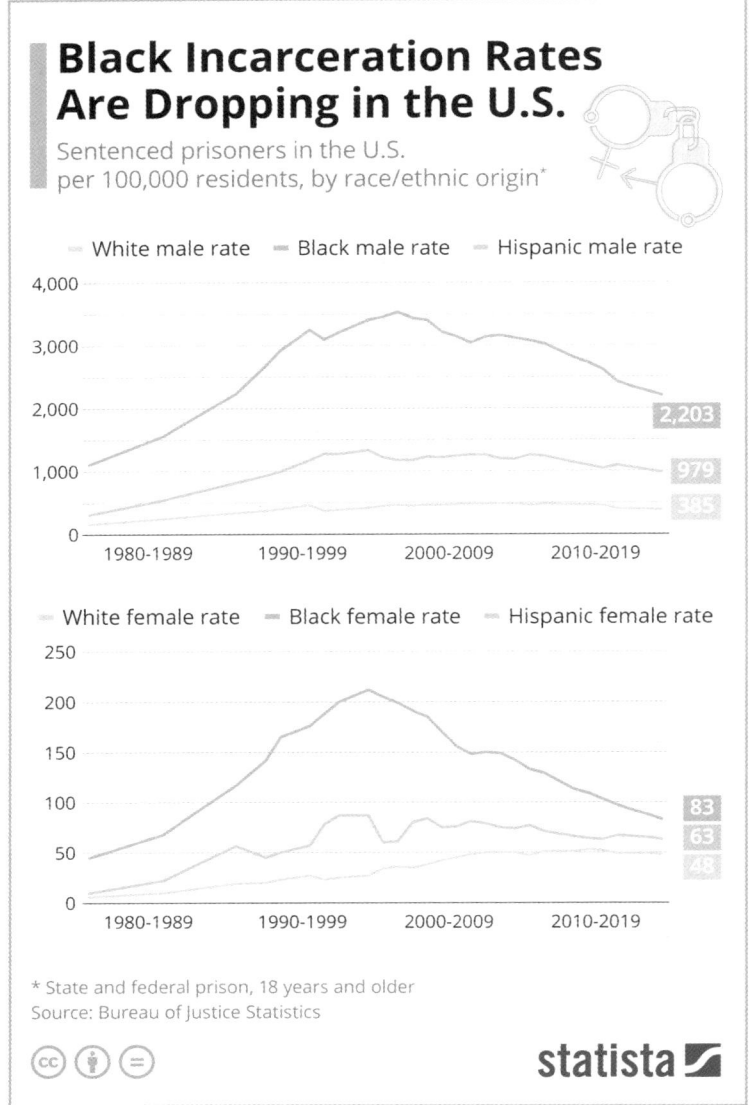

Black Incarceration Rates Are Dropping in the U.S.

Sentenced prisoners in the U.S.
per 100,000 residents, by race/ethnic origin*

— White male rate — Black male rate — Hispanic male rate

2,203
979
385

1980-1989   1990-1999   2000-2009   2010-2019

— White female rate — Black female rate — Hispanic female rate

83
63
48

1980-1989   1990-1999   2000-2009   2010-2019

* State and federal prison, 18 years and older
Source: Bureau of Justice Statistics

statista ⚡

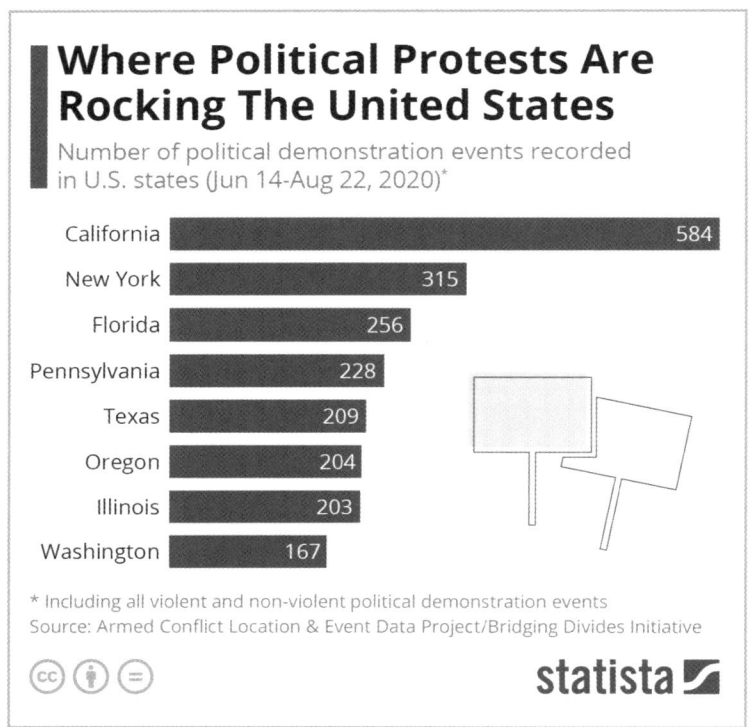

Where Political Protests Are Rocking The United States

Number of political demonstration events recorded
in U.S. states (Jun 14-Aug 22, 2020)*

California	584
New York	315
Florida	256
Pennsylvania	228
Texas	209
Oregon	204
Illinois	203
Washington	167

* Including all violent and non-violent political demonstration events
Source: Armed Conflict Location & Event Data Project/Bridging Divides Initiative

statista ⚡

Largest Companies Pledge Over $1.6 Billion to Fight Inequality

Amount of money pledged by each Fortune 100 company to fight inequality since George Floyd's death (in millions)

Company	Amount	Ranking
Bank of America	$1,000	25
Walmart	$100	1
Comcast	$100	28
Apple	$100	4
Anthem	$50	29
Nike	$40	85
Alphabet	$38	11
Other (35)	$202	

Sources: Fortune 500, Axios

statista

Do Americans Support Changes in Police Spending?

Percentage of U.S. adults who believe spending on policing should increase, decrease or stay the same

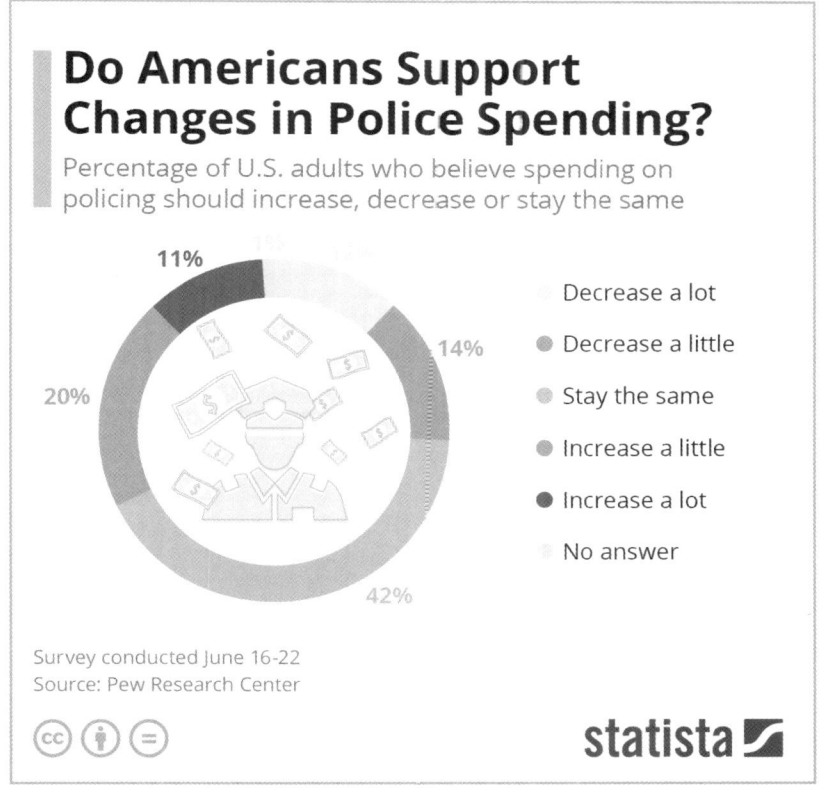

11%
14%
20%
42%

- Decrease a lot
- Decrease a little
- Stay the same
- Increase a little
- Increase a lot
- No answer

Survey conducted June 16-22
Source: Pew Research Center

statista

| Graphics: *Statista*

51

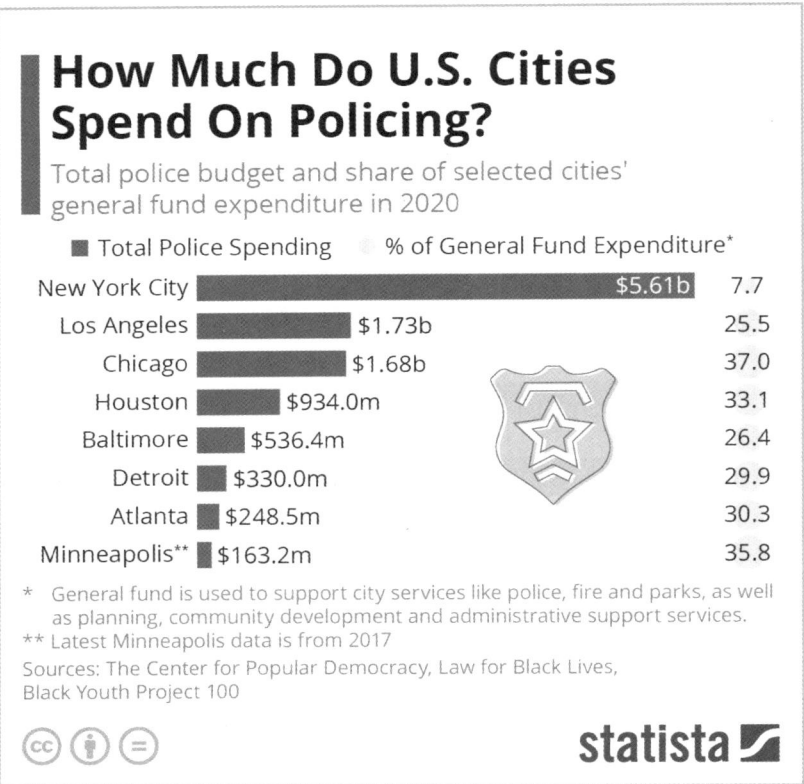

How Much Do U.S. Cities Spend On Policing?

Total police budget and share of selected cities' general fund expenditure in 2020

■ Total Police Spending   ⬤ % of General Fund Expenditure*

City	Total Police Spending	% of General Fund Expenditure*
New York City	$5.61b	7.7
Los Angeles	$1.73b	25.5
Chicago	$1.68b	37.0
Houston	$934.0m	33.1
Baltimore	$536.4m	26.4
Detroit	$330.0m	29.9
Atlanta	$248.5m	30.3
Minneapolis**	$163.2m	35.8

*   General fund is used to support city services like police, fire and parks, as well as planning, community development and administrative support services.
** Latest Minneapolis data is from 2017

Sources: The Center for Popular Democracy, Law for Black Lives, Black Youth Project 100

statista 🇿

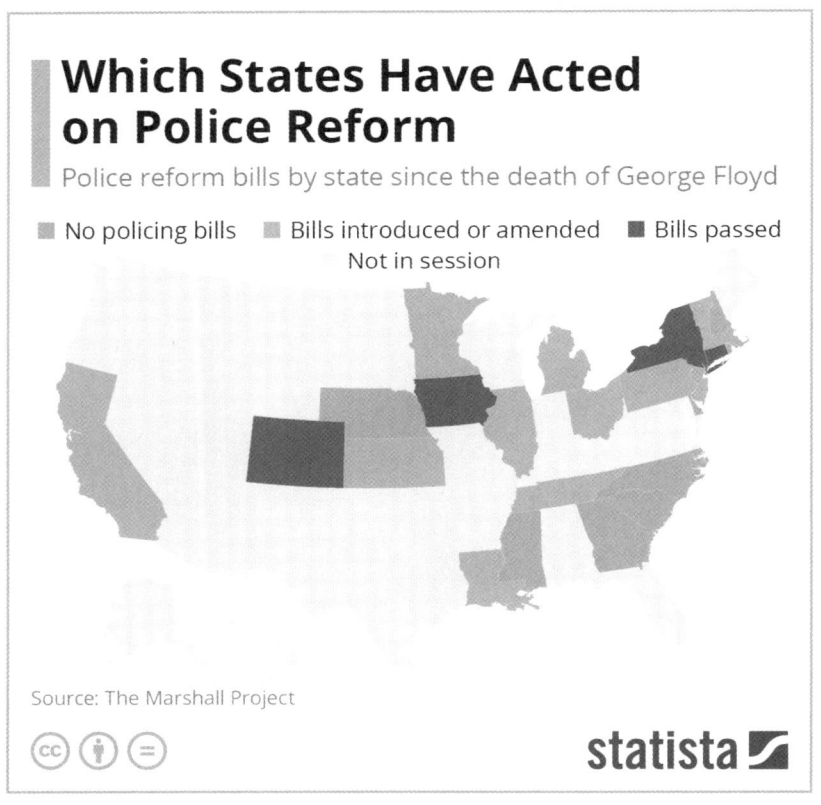

Which States Have Acted on Police Reform

Police reform bills by state since the death of George Floyd

■ No policing bills   ■ Bills introduced or amended   ■ Bills passed
Not in session

Source: The Marshall Project

statista 🇿

| GRAPHICS: *Statista*

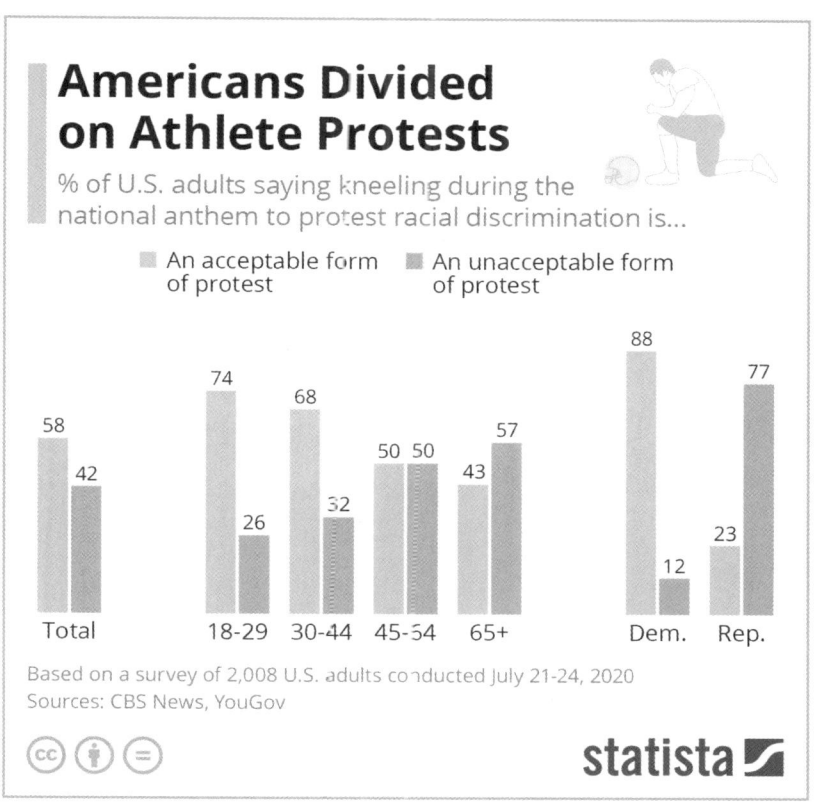

Americans Divided on Athlete Protests

% of U.S. adults saying kneeling during the national anthem to protest racial discrimination is...

An acceptable form of protest   An unacceptable form of protest

Total: 58, 42
18-29: 74, 26
30-44: 68, 32
45-64: 50, 50
65+: 43, 57
Dem.: 88, 12
Rep.: 23, 77

Based on a survey of 2,008 U.S. adults conducted July 21-24, 2020
Sources: CBS News, YouGov

statista

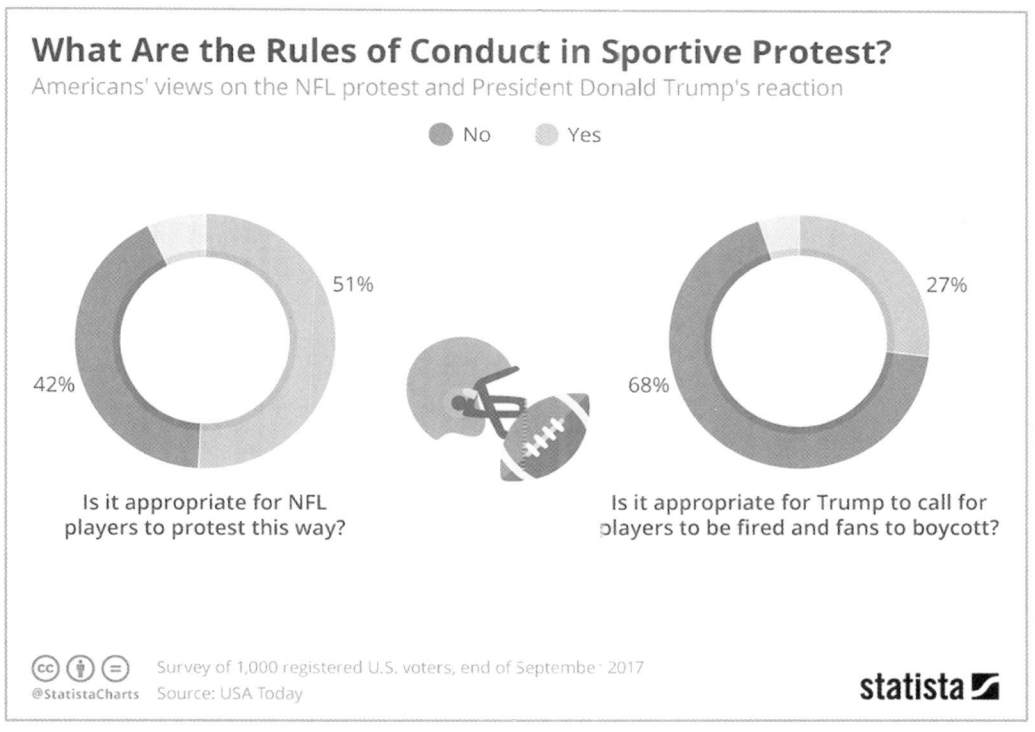

What Are the Rules of Conduct in Sportive Protest?

Americans' views on the NFL protest and President Donald Trump's reaction

No   Yes

Is it appropriate for NFL players to protest this way? — 51% / 42%

Is it appropriate for Trump to call for players to be fired and fans to boycott? — 27% / 68%

Survey of 1,000 registered U.S. voters, end of September 2017
@StatistaCharts   Source: USA Today

statista

GRAPHICS: *Statista*

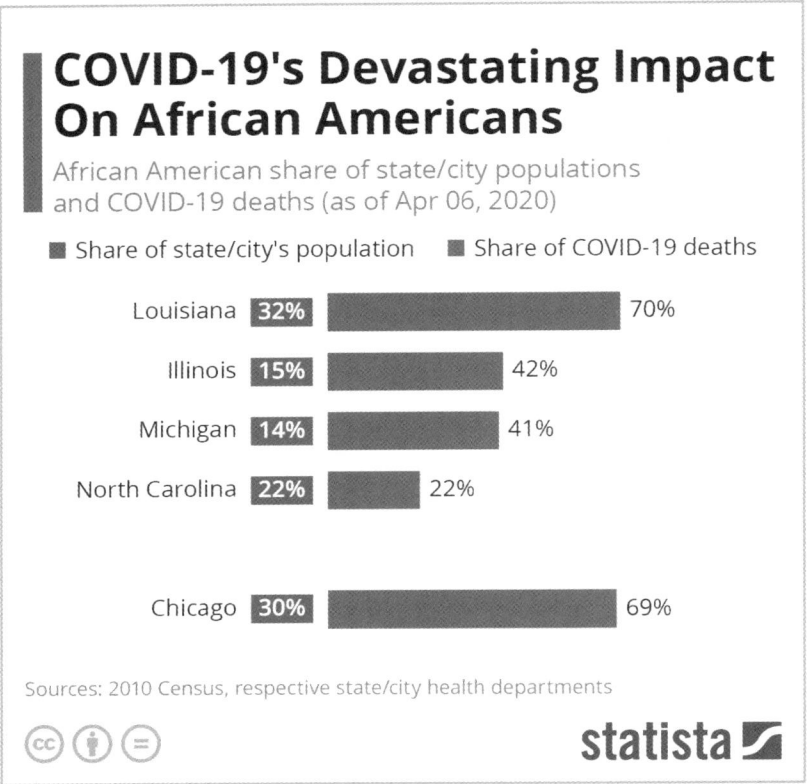

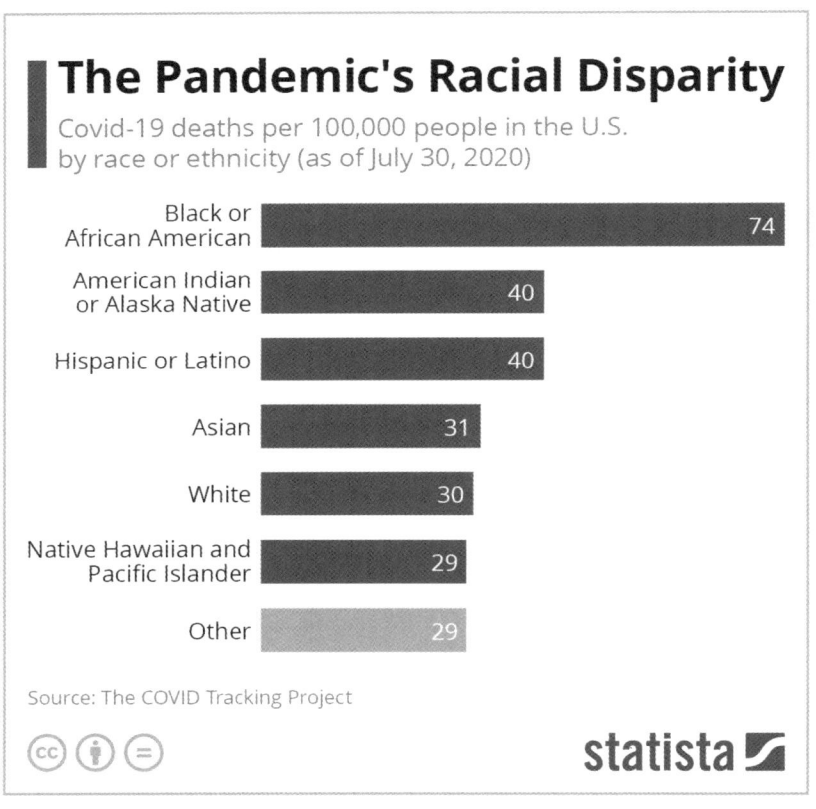

GRAPHICS: *Statista*

Using Social Media for Political Issues

Percentage of social media users who say each aspect of social media is important to them

- Finding others who share views on important issues
- Getting involved in issues important to them
- Giving them a venue to express political opinions

Black
60% 60% 51%

Hispanic
57% 53% 53%

White
39% 37% 34%

Survey conducted June 16-22
Source: Pew Research Center

cc (i) (=)

statista ⚏

The Gender Pay Gap Visualized

Gender pay gaps and equal pay days for different races and ethnicities in the U.S.

For every dollar white, non-Hispanic men earned in 2018, women were paid...

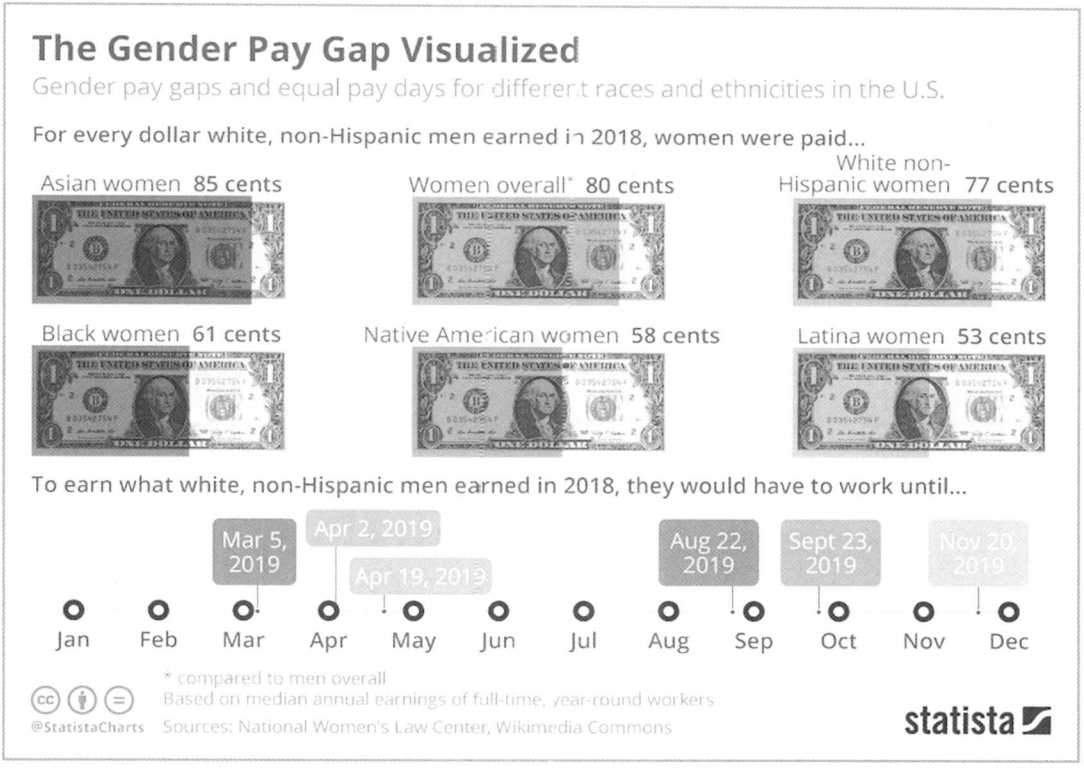

Asian women 85 cents

Women overall* 80 cents

White non-Hispanic women 77 cents

Black women 61 cents

Native American women 58 cents

Latina women 53 cents

To earn what white, non-Hispanic men earned in 2018, they would have to work until...

Mar 5, 2019 — Apr 2, 2019 — Apr 19, 2019 — Aug 22, 2019 — Sept 23, 2019 — Nov 20, 2019

Jan Feb Mar Apr May Jun Jul Aug Sep Oct Nov Dec

* compared to men overall
Based on median annual earnings of full-time, year-round workers
@StatistaCharts   Sources: National Women's Law Center, Wikimedia Commons

cc (i) (=)

statista ⚏

1. Auflage 2024 23 22 21

Alle Drucke dieser Auflage sind unverändert und können im
Unterricht nebeneinander verwendet werden. Die letzte Zahl bezeichnet
das Jahr des Drucks.

www.schuenemann-verlag.de | www.sprachzeitungen.de

Redaktion: Katrin Günther, Carol Richards, Anne-Kathrein Schiffer

Gestaltung und Satz: Britta Leuchtmann, Christoph Lück

Abbildungen Umschlag: Vorderseite, S. 43: Getty Images
von links nach rechts: Getty Images, Picture Alliance, Picture Alliance
Rückseite, von links nach rechts: Picture Alliance, Getty Images,
Picture Alliance/Reuters

Printed in EU 2021 | ISBN 978-3-7961-1077-1